Rick Pogue

Risk is a Four Letter Word

The Asset Allocation Approach to Investing

George Hartman

Stoddart

Published in 1994 by
Stoddart Publishing Co. Limited
34 Lesmill Road
Don Mills, Ontario
M3B 2T6
(416) 445-3333

Fourth printing December 1995

First published in 1992 by
Hartman & Company Inc.

Canadian Cataloguing in Publication Data

Hartman, George E. (George Edward), 1949–
Risk is a four letter word

ISBN 0-7737-5662-0

1. Finance, Personal.   2. Finance, Personal — Canada.
3. Investments — Canada.   4. Risk.   I. Title.

HG179.H37 1994   332.024   C94-930895-1

Editor: Linda Kenyon, Kenyon & Company
Design: Ray Squirrel/Scott McMann

Printed and bound in Canada

Stoddart Publishing gratefully acknowledges the support
of the Canada Council, Ontario Ministry of Culture,
Tourism, and Recreation, Ontario Arts Council, and
Ontario Publishing Centre in the development of writing
and publishing in Canada.

To Janie

Contents

THERE ARE RISKS AND COSTS TO A PROGRAM OF ACTION.
BUT THEY ARE FAR LESS THAN THE LONG-RANGE RISKS AND
COSTS OF COMFORTABLE INACTION.
–JOHN F. KENNEDY

Foreword

There is no such thing as a riskless investment. And common sense would dictate that if there was, it wouldn't offer sufficient returns to justify buying it.

There's the rub.

Risk and reward are closely linked. For the most part, the higher an investment's perceived risk, the higher its potential reward. Therefore, attempting to eliminate or even to dramatically reduce risk may not be an investor's most prudent strategy.

Am I suggesting that an investor should wholeheartedly embrace risk? No. Although theoretically that approach may lead to fine long-term performance, when mixed with human nature, it often self-destructs. For with increased risk comes increased volatility. And with increased volatility comes increased stress. And with increased stress comes an increased number of emotional decisions. And that final increase leads to Canadians' favourite investment practice – "buy high, sell low" (or to my family's traditional version – "buy extremely high, sell extremely low").

So the answer, for most of us, can be found neither by shunning risk nor by marrying it. Instead we should court it – learn to accept it, work with it, and most important, strive to understand it.

How much risk is acceptable? How much is prudent? Of course, the answer differs for each of us depending on a number of factors including our risk-tolerance level, the desired rewards, and our time-frame.

How we best allocate our assets must take these factors into account as well as some others, for example, whether we want to actively or passively manage our money. That's what this book is all about. Not giving you a prescribed asset mix, but instead teaching you how to develop your own strategy, one you can understand, feel comfortable with, maintain, and prosper from.

Asset allocation is not the same as market-timing. That's a good thing because all empirical evidence indicates accurate market-timing is a pipe-dream. Instead, George Hartman's approach to asset allocation teaches the judicious management of risk through diversification – a worthy objective for all of us.

Dave Chilton
The Wealthy Barber

Acknowledgements

After many years of lecturing on the subject of investing, I assumed that putting the concepts I'd so often presented into written form would be a relatively easy task. I quickly learned, however, that it was far from easy and impossible to do alone. A book such as this would not have happened without the assistance and encouragement of many people.

I am very grateful to David Chilton, author of the enormously successful *The Wealthy Barber*, who first showed how anxious the Canadian public is for common sense ideas about financial planning and investing. David's encouragement and criticism always seemed to come at precisely the right time. I am honoured to have the foreword to this book written by David.

The initial idea for this book came from my exposure to two other authors and lecturers. They are Roger Gibson *(Asset Allocation: Balancing Financial Risk)* and Michael Hirsch *(Multifund Investing: How To Build a High Performance Portfolio of Mutual Funds)*. I first became acquainted with both of these gentlemen at meetings of the International Association for Financial Planning and would now count myself among their most devoted disciples.

I am grateful to my long-time friend Everett Banning who had the courage to sit me down one day and tell me what he thought was wrong with the book. The result is much better because of that afternoon.

My former business colleagues at the Universal Group deserve special mention: Laurie Paul, who not only encouraged me but also covered for me when my attention was more on the book than my job; Gail Wright, whose persistence in asking "When?" kept me writing when I'd rather have been golfing; David Riddle, who brought a professional investment advisor's insight to the content; and particularly Bill Holland, who so enthusiastically introduced me to new sources of information and whose own original thoughts helped focus some of mine.

Of course, no author could fail to acknowledge the unsung hero of any book – the editor. It must be one of the most difficult jobs in the world, telling someone who thinks they have described something in the wittiest or the most profound way possible that it could be done better and then showing them how. Linda Kenyon is a professional in every regard.

My thanks go out to the many financial planners and investment advisors and their clients across the country who have listened to my dissertations on asset allocation. Through dialog with them, I have learned to differentiate between what is theoretical and what is practical.

And finally to Jane, who has been there at every turn. She is my motivation and my inspiration and the person to whom this book is dedicated.

BECAUSE INVESTING IS AN INEXACT SCIENCE, IT IS BETTER
TO BE APPROXIMATELY RIGHT THAN PRECISELY WRONG.

Introduction

This is a book about concepts. Some are original, but many are borrowed, because after 20 years in the financial services industry, I can
confidently say that when it comes to investing, everyone has an opinion.
Unfortunately with the multitude of opinions come many misconcep-
tions. Investment portfolios are often made up of assets that are
"comfortable" rather than appropriate. The good news is that by learning
a few basic truths about the behaviour of investment markets, you can
apply the same principles to your individual portfolio that professional
money managers use for billion dollar accounts.

The evolution in thinking about investment strategy over the last
two decades has been fascinating. It is only within the past few years, for
example, that the term "asset allocation" has become part of the financial
vocabulary. Traditionally, we have been taught to avoid "putting all our
eggs in one basket." The present-day view of diversification goes consid-
erably beyond having more than one basket; today's strategy is to use a
number of baskets, each with different contents, that is, investments with
varying patterns of return. The story of "modern portfolio theory" began

1

with the simple assumption by Noble Prize winner Harry Markowitz that, as investors, we *like* potential return and *dislike* risk. Therefore the thrust of modern portfolio theory is to shift emphasis away from trying to maximize return to trying to manage risk. The goal is no longer to try to beat the market, but rather to devise long term strategies to move you toward your financial objectives with the least amount of risk. Asset allocation does not try to outguess the investment markets so much as it intelligently works with them.

As we progress, I will draw on the concepts of modern portfolio theory but only to the extent that they help us understand asset allocation. The emphasis will be on developing a practical framework for making investment decisions that will give you confidence in the choices you have made and reduce the temptation to change them during market fluctuations.

As you read through this book you might be surprised to discover that there are many places where I am not very precise. That's because I want to avoid getting lost in charts, graphs and "number crunching" which is so easy to do when discussing investment strategy. The data from which some of the strategies are derived is very comprehensive but I have done most of the work in extracting what we need and have tried to present the relevant information in a useful format. Precision is less important than conceptual understanding because in the broad scheme of investing, there is no such thing as the perfect plan. One minute after you have made an investment decision, it is almost a sure bet that the world will not have unfolded exactly as you predicted. Stock markets will have misbehaved, interest rates will have risen or fallen more or less than expected, your financial objectives will have changed or your attitude towards certain investment options will be different.

Because of these evolving influences, investment decision making is not a "do it once and forget about it" proposition. Through your lifetime, you will make thousands of choices that will have an impact on your financial well-being. The best you can hope for is to make the most sound judgements you can, based on the best information you have available at the time. When things change along the way, as they inevitably will, you must re-examine your earlier decisions to see if they are still appropriate.

Doesn't that make the whole exercise futile? No, because to do nothing in the way of investment planning would be a much greater mistake than to have used assumptions that ultimately proved to be slightly inaccurate. I know this won't please the more analytical among you, but my objective is to develop an investment strategy that is *approximately right rather than precisely wrong.*

Let me also acknowledge that there are many well-trained financial planners, tax experts and investment professionals out there who can provide sound advice in their respective disciplines. In fact, quite frequently throughout this book, you'll see phrases like, "Consult an expert" and, indeed, you'll find numerous comments from the experts I've encountered over the years. So the logical question is, "What gives this guy the right to write about investment strategies? Is he some kind of guru who has made millions with his magic formula?"

The answer to that one is "No." First, there is no "magic" and secondly, you will derive your own formula from the concepts presented. And while my own investment portfolio is largely doing what I'd hoped it would, that does not give me authority to suggest how others might meet their own financial objectives. My "licence," so-to-speak, comes from *observation.* In the course of my day-to-day activities, I have the privilege of dealing with the very best professional money managers, financial planners, investment advisors and client service people in the country. I have spoken to thousands of investors at public seminars, in classrooms, at investment shows, in large and small groups and one-on-one. From these collected experiences have emerged a number of common yet seldom expressed themes – dealing with the "human" side of investing. So that's what this book is about – not the "psychology of investing" but investing for psychological comfort, for *a piece of the action with peace of mind.*

To accomplish the task, I have divided the book into three parts. Part I could be considered "mental preparation" because it describes our human frailties as investors. We often make irrational decisions even when we are aware of the less-than-desirable consequences. Recognizing the weaknesses of human nature, however, goes a long way towards minimizing the damage we might do to our investment portfolios. We know, for example, that the greatest fear of most investors is having their assets decline in value, so we seek out "safe" investments to avoid volatility. Unfortunately, the types of investments that don't fluctuate in value typically do a very poor job of keeping pace with inflation. So to the extent we try to battle volatility, we expose ourselves to inflation.

Structuring a portfolio to find an equilibrium between the competing risks of volatility and inflation is the objective of Part II. It might best be described as the "how to" section because it takes the theories developed in Part I and presents a framework for applying them. By the time you have finished this part of the book, you will have a written Investment Statement that will guide you and any advisors you may enlist through the asset allocation approach to investing. It will enable you to design your portfolio so that it reflects your personal philosophy, balances risk and reward and gives you the ability to realize your financial objectives. Be cautioned, however, that I am not going to provide all the answers as to how you can be successful as an investor. My job is to ask the questions. It will be your responses that turn the theories into practical applications. Finally, Part III is a discussion of the merits of mutual funds. I don't know of a more appropriate vehicle for carrying out the strategies we will be developing throughout the book so I have devoted a fair bit of space to them.

There is a lot of ground to cover so let's get started by considering, for a moment, the way we think, feel and behave as investors. In this regard, I have come to the following conclusion: people want to behave rationally when it comes to investing but *human nature* gets in the way.

Summary

- *Investors often have portfolios that are "comfortable" rather than appropriate.*
- *The basic truths about investing that professional money managers use can be applied to individual investors' portfolios.*
- Asset allocation *goes beyond the traditional view of diversification.*
- *Asset allocation does not attempt to outguess the markets so much as it intelligently works with them.*
- *By combining assets with different performance characteristics into a single portfolio, it is possible to increase return and reduce risk.*
- *Because investing is an inexact science, it is better to be* approximately right than precisely wrong *in your choices.*

Chapter One:

We Have Met the Enemy – He Is US

"WE HAVE MET THE ENEMY... AND HE IS US!"
–POGO

The Human Nature of Investors

Ah, Pogo – one of my favourite philosophers! Certainly he is more widely read than most, and as trite as the musings of a comic strip character may seem to us, I believe Pogo is right. Much of the grief we experience as investors is self-inflicted. We do our best to make it difficult to succeed in investing – not because we want to, just because we are human. That means we all have feelings, attitudes, desires, beliefs and biases and are capable of judging and second-guessing. To attempt to build an investment portfolio without considering what makes us different from one another would be comparable to my taking medicine prescribed by your doctor for you. I may have some of the same symptoms but chances are the cause, the ailment itself or at least my reaction to the medicine would be quite different.

For example, how we respond as individuals to opportunities or crises has a significant bearing on how we should structure our investment portfolios. This is not to suggest that successful investing means managing a series of calamities or pouncing with split-second timing and precision on unexpected opportunities. Quite the contrary, the strategies

I am going to propose are designed to eliminate the need for hasty decision-making, but spontaneity does play a part.

In fact, the most revealing aspect of our "investor psychology" is the extent to which we are predictable. For many, the sheer complexity – the length and breadth of the investment decision-making process – is over-whelming. As a consequence, we tend to follow patterns. To a surprisingly large extent, we rely on other people for advice, even if the closest we've ever come to witnessing the money management skill of that individual was watching how well he or she handled the gratuity when we were last out to dinner. So golf courses, health clubs, beauty salons, cocktail parties and even public transit become our classrooms for learning investment strategies.

We are also very much affected by our most recent experience. If we have made money "flipping" houses during hot real estate markets, we are sure we can do it at least once more. Conversely, if the stock market has been unkind to us, it may be quite a while before we'll venture into that arena again. The high returns of the past few years on bonds, money market mutual funds and GICs have some people convinced that those are the only investments to own. The list is endless. For every conceivable investment, there is someone with a success story and someone with a tale of woe.

There is another common facet of our investment psyche that merits mention. We like to invest in things we can see or touch and, if possible, show off to our friends. We'll park that shiny new (rapidly depreciating) car in the driveway for all the neighbours to see. But will we call our friends to tell them one of our mutual funds just went up 10 cents? As Jim Lawton, Senior Partner with Lawton Partners Financial Planning of Winnipeg tells his clients, "My competition for your money is not the banks or other investment institutions – it's General Motors! And that's not fair because they have a much larger advertising budget than I do. They are in your home, on television every night. But if we want to meet your financial objectives, I've got to get you to invest with me rather than GM – that's tough because GM has taught you to love them and hate me!" Or as well-known U.S. investment commentator, Michael Lipper says, "All investors need 'bragging rights'." So while all the investment choices we make may not be the most appropriate for us, our psychological attitude towards them will play an important role in our "comfort level." And our degree of comfort with our assets will influence the extent to which we are willing to hold onto them through bad times while waiting for prices to rise or to sell them in good times to realize our profits.

Furthermore, most of us view investments as stand-alone transactions, not as part of an overall strategy or program. And because we are natural procrastinators when it comes to investment decisions, we choose the easy way out: parking our money in places we perceive to be "safe" with the occasional (usually painful) foray into something more exotic that came to us over the tinkle of ice cubes at the company Christmas party or from our spouse's second cousin who is now "in the business" of whatever.

But let's not be too hard on ourselves. Keep in mind that we have a great deal more to contend with in our day-to-day lives than just our investments. We have jobs, family and social activities and the "worries of the world" occupying our thoughts. We are also being constantly bombarded with information – in newspapers, magazines, radio, television and even mail drops through the door! When we couple this mountain of data with a dearth of time to focus on things like choosing investments, it is no wonder we allow ourselves to be pushed farther down the path of least resistance. Because we lack the clearness of mind, the opportunity or the capability to make timely decisions, we opt for simple, low-risk investments. We do this in spite of the fact that we understand that higher returns are possible with only small increases in "risk" and that, as rational investors, we should seek to balance risk and reward more judiciously.

Obviously every investor does not react in the ways I have described, but enough do to say there is some commonality. Regardless, however, of our own investment personality, there are certain "truths" that affect us all. The most important one for us to accept is the inviolate investment axiom that *low-risk investments yield only low rates of return and higher returns are only achieved by moving to a higher level of risk.* Furthermore, both risk and reward are time dependent. As time progresses, low-yielding investments become more risky, because of inflation. On the other hand, the returns associated with higher-risk investments become more stable and predictable over time, thereby reducing the level of risk. I'll make this clear with some specific examples later. Before I do so, however, let me highlight the two key words that will form the foundation for much of this book: *risk* and *reward.* For this is what investing is all about – the "trade-off" between the opportunity to earn higher returns and the consequences of trying to do so. We will get to the reward part soon enough. But now, let's spend the next chapter exploring the nature of that ugly monster called "risk" a little more deeply.

Summary

- *Investors want to behave rationally, but* human nature *gets in the way.*
- *Because we lack the clearness of mind, the opportunity or the capability to make timely decisions, we opt for simple, low-risk investments.*
- *There is an inviolate investment axiom that low-risk investments yield only low rates of return and higher returns are only achieved by moving to a higher level of risk.*
- *Both risk and reward are time dependent. As time progresses, inflation makes low-yielding investments more risky while higher-risk investments become more stable and predictable over time.*

Chapter Two:
RISK Is a Four Letter Word

THERE IS NO SUCH THING AS A RISK-FREE INVESTMENT.
THE CHALLENGE IS TO DECIDE WHAT LEVEL OF RISK
YOU ARE WILLING TO ASSUME AND TO UNDERSTAND THE
IMPLICATIONS OF THAT CHOICE.

Risk-Free Investments

It continues to amaze me how, despite their increasing sophistication, investors (and advisors) are reluctant to talk or write about risk. It is as if uttering the word itself will bring certain disaster to an investment. Frequently, when I am scheduled to speak at a seminar (usually sponsored by a financial planner or an investment advisor), I'll receive a telephone call a few days before the event, that goes something like this: "I heard that when you spoke for old Charlie over in Red Deer last year, you spent an awful lot of time talking about 'risk.' My clients are fairly conservative. They don't like risk. Could you maybe 'soft peddle' that risk stuff... please?"

The answer to that one is easy: No! We can't talk about the rewards of investing without laying bare the risks involved. They are inseparable. And even more importantly, *there is no such thing as a risk-free investment!* I can't tell you how many times I have been at a social gathering and when someone learns that I have something to do with the investment business, have been asked the inevitable question, "What can I invest in over the next year that will give me a high return but has no risk?" My answer is "I don't know, but if you find out, don't tell anyone else – except me!"

Risk wears many disguises and in one way or another has an impact on every investment alternative. If you as an investor decide to bury your money in your garden or even leave it in the bank, you have to accept the very low probability of real capital growth. Even a decision to do nothing is very important in its impact on a portfolio's performance. Many investors in bonds, for example, have been surprised to learn that these fixed income investments decline in value as interest rates change. And, of course, there are the risks associated with the stock market and real estate and the liquidity and tax risk of limited partnerships and so on.

So the real task is not to try to find "risk-free" investments – there aren't any. The challenge is to decide what *level of risk* you are willing to assume and then, having decided on your risk tolerance, to understand the *implications of that choice.*

Risk = Potential for Loss

So here is the very first assignment in preparing yourself psychologically to invest: to determine your "risk tolerance." This is such a fundamental and important part of the foundation to a successful investment strategy that we are going to spend several chapters doing it. But first, let's start with a definition of the word "risk" itself by simply saying that "risk is the potential for *loss.*" Well if, as the title of this book and chapter suggests, *risk* is a four letter word, then certainly *loss* is even more profane. At least "risk" implies some possibility of gain; "loss" says, "The game is over – it's gone!"

Now wait a minute, you say. Why are we dwelling on this risk/loss thing so much? It surely doesn't create a positive attitude towards investing, does it? The reason is that investors' attitudes have shifted sharply over the past few years – to be more precise, ever since Monday, October 19, 1987. The stock market "crash" of 1987 changed the way people perceived risk. Prior to that event, a "rational investor" was one who, according to the textbooks, sought to avoid *risk*. From Tuesday, October 20, 1987 on, the rational investor became one who sought to avoid *loss!* In fact, it would be fair to say that the true rational investor, the one who will accept higher risk if assured of higher returns is indeed, a rare breed — difficult to find today. We have discovered that as investors, we are psychologically far more fragile than we thought. The consequence is that we now find more comfort in lower, predictable returns than in higher but more volatile ones. As prices of stocks, bonds, real estate, gold, oil or whatever have become increasingly unstable, we are now as concerned with the return *of* our money as we are interested in the return *on* our money.

And with that, we've led ourselves right up to one of the fundamental components of risk: *volatility*, or as I'd prefer to call it, the "fluctuation factor."

Volatility

Although we have always known, for example, that stock markets move up and down, this volatility has not been a major concern for most Canadians because about 85 percent of their investments were in other than stocks, most typically in bank accounts, GICs and Canada Savings Bonds. As long as interest rates did not fluctuate too much, these types of investments were fairly "comforting." But let's take a closer look at what has happened to interest rates. In the graph that follows, I have used the returns over a forty-three year period for Treasury Bills and bonds issued by the Government of Canada to illustrate interest rate trends. Don't worry too much about the absolute numbers: first look at the left half of the graph, which covers the period from 1951 to about 1970. There you see that, although interest rates did fluctuate, they did so in a fairly predictable manner and within a moderate range of, say, 10 to 15 percent. Now look at the right half of the graph, representing the most recent twenty years, and note the difference. From the early 1970s on, the range of return is doubled. Volatility has become a real factor for even the most conservative investors.

Annual Price Changes (1951-1993)

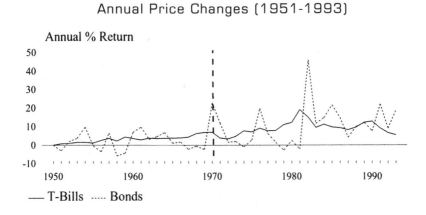

— T-Bills ····· Bonds

Now let's look at the stock market by superimposing its returns on the same graph. I have used the Toronto Stock Exchange Index to represent stock price changes.

Annual Price Changes (1951-1993)

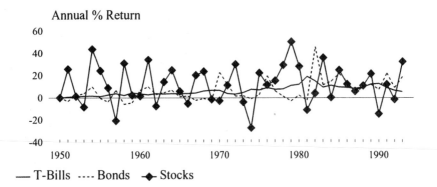

— T-Bills ···· Bonds ◆ Stocks

No surprises here – stock markets have always been volatile! They change direction, not in years or months or weeks, but recently, in days or even hours! Ah yes, you say, that makes my case for putting my money in those low-risk, interest-generating assets like GICs, term deposits and Treasury Bills to reduce the "fluctuation factor" even stronger. Not necessarily so! Whereas in earlier times we could have felt reasonably confident about locking money into GICs for, say, five years, there have been several periods in our recent history when that would have been a mistake. How would you feel about having bought a five-year GIC yielding 12 percent interest and then one year later having interest rates climb to 20 percent? If your money hadn't been locked in for five years, you might have been able to reinvest it at the then current rates and increase your return by more than 60 percent! That's exactly the situation we lived through in 1980 to 1982. More recently, we saw short-term yields increase by more than 40 percent between 1988 and 1990.

Does that mean we shouldn't buy GICs with five-year maturities? Again, not necessarily. Under normal conditions, the longer you tie your money up, the better the rate of return you should expect, because, as we have just seen, *the risk is higher.* But in Canada, we have, several times in the past 20 years, experienced "inverted yield curves" where short-term interest rates were higher than long-term rates. And similar things have happened with other investments, for example, real estate. Who in Vancouver, Calgary, Toronto or Montreal does not have a tale of woe, their own or a friend's, regarding skyrocketing then plummeting real estate prices? The point I am trying to make is that *all* investments fluctuate in value or relative rate of return. It doesn't matter if we are talking about stocks, bonds, money market instruments, real estate, artwork, the family jewels or Grandpa's farm. There are times when each one appears to be either a better or worse investment than the others. Volatility of value is common to them all.

So the first major component of risk is volatility: the "fluctuation factor." Let's move on to number two, the one we all know so well yet forget so easily.

Inflation – The "Double Demon"

I have often described inflation as a "double demon" because it affects our financial resources in two very negative ways. First, it depletes accumulated capital, that is, it destroys wealth. Secondly and perhaps more devastatingly from the perspective of most investors, it reduces the purchasing power of income. I'll illustrate both these points in a moment. Before I do, however, I'd like to say a little more about inflation and our psychological reaction to it.

The major problem with the inflation issue is not so much how it ravages wealth (as deadly serious as that is). No, it is the way we have come to accept inflation as "normal" and inevitable. Why? Because most of us have never lived without it. In fact, for most readers of this book, any inflation figure around six percent is pretty much "okay." It's acceptable because when we first began to accumulate assets in a significant way, it was in the late 1970s into early 1980s and during those years, inflation averaged around eight to ten percent, peaking at over 12 percent in 1982. It has generally been declining since then and despite the best efforts of governments around the world to beat inflation all the way down to zero, few of us actually believe it will get there or persist. An annual inflation rate of five to seven percent would keep most of us happy – even though deep down we probably agree it should be lower.

Obviously not everyone reading this will have been born between 1947 and 1966, will have dependents and an established career, will own property and will be an investor. However, most of you will.

How do I know? Demographics!

And you thought this was a book about investing for maximum return with peace of mind! Well, it is. But demographics, the study of people and their numbers, play a very large role, and the simple truth is that the majority of Canadians who are interested in investing (and would, therefore, buy or borrow this book) are between the ages of 25 and 45. That age group also exhibits the greatest incidence of the other characteristics I mentioned.

I am, of course, referring to the so-called "baby boom" generation. I'm one of them, except that now we have become the "baby bulge." While that may aptly describe the physical appearance of some of us, to the demographer it simply means that we were born in the few years following World War II. We now represent the largest segment of the Canadian population and, like a lump moving through a snake, we are getting towards the tail end of the age distribution. That's a polite way of saying we are getting older. The members of this group are generally now well settled in terms of occupation and lifestyle. We are in our peak earning years and very interested in accumulating assets to be used later to provide income. Whereas a few years ago, we were primarily consumption oriented — buying goods and services to enhance our standard of living — we are now increasingly aware of the need to build wealth for eventual retirement. We have made the psychological shift from being "spenders" to being "savers."

Our interest in financial affairs is also markedly higher than it generally was for our parents for two more reasons. First, in most cases, there has been a significant increase in the number and types of financial assets within our individual control. Now we simply have to make a greater variety of investment decisions. This has come about largely through the popularity and growth of Registered Retirement Savings Plans (RRSPs). Secondly, the most recent ten years have seen the highest overall rates of return in history for just about every commonly used investment. The consequence is that there has been, in most cases, a substantial increase in the market value of those financial assets since we began to accumulate them. We are now far more affluent, on average, than our peers were a decade ago, so naturally we are more interested in asset management.

But what has all this to do with the risk of inflation? It seems so long ago we started talking about it, doesn't it?

Recall my statement earlier that many of us will accept a five to seven percent inflation rate as "normal." That's because we grew up, so to speak, with much higher annual cost-of-living hikes and we survived. In the most recent past, however, as inflation has tumbled, we have been lulled into thinking it might not be a problem anymore. In 1993, for example, the Consumer Price Index showed a gain of only 1.7 percent, so many of us have pushed it to the back of our minds as a concern. I believe, however, such thinking could lead to a serious underestimation of the long-term impact of inflation.

Despite the published rate of inflation being less than 2 percent, I still saw my hydro-electric bill increase by about 8 percent, my automobile insurance by almost 11 percent; my income tax by 7 percent; my health care costs by similar amounts and, worst of all, my golf club fees went up by 10 percent! My personal rate of inflation seems to be much higher than 1.7 percent and I suspect if you think about the goods and services you consume, you may discover the same thing.

The other nasty thing about inflation, besides its familiarity breeding complacency, is that it is insidious. It sneaks up on us: we don't even know it has been until after it's gone. That's because it weaves its way into everything — wages, prices, interest rates, stock returns, real estate values — everything. I like the way Ed Morrow of Confidential Planning Services in Middletown, Ohio, one of the United States' best known financial planners, describes inflation. He calls it "Robin Hood in reverse" — more like a "Robbing Hood." It takes not from the wealthy, but from the poor and those just starting their economic life. And it pays the wealthy, those who own real estate and businesses.

So what is the point of all this? Even though we are currently experiencing a downtrend, inflation will return! No one can say exactly when, but it is a fact that there have been inflationary cycles throughout the recorded history of mankind — in all parts of the globe. Inflation is like an old alarm clock. It sits beside your bed, facing the other way, ticking away. You can't read the time but sooner or later, it will go off with a jarring noise that will jangle your nerves. You'll want to reach out to push in the alarm button to stop all the racket.

So how do we push the button on inflation? By carefully investing in assets which traditionally grow at a rate greater than inflation. And that means equity-type investments as compared to debt or cash instruments, such as mortgages, term deposits, bonds and bank accounts. As Ted Thomson, Chairman of the Financial Concept Group in North Bay, Ontario, so evangelically preaches, "Be an *owner* – not a *loaner.*"

One could leap to the conclusion that I have just advocated pulling all your money out of banks and plunging into the stock market. That would be both wrong and completely contrary to what we are actually trying to accomplish here: to develop a strategy which generates "maximum return with peace of mind." What I am saying is that, for most investors, inflation is often a grossly underestimated risk. I just want to be sure that when the inflation Robin Hood returns, you won't be an unwary traveller – you'll own a piece of the forest!

The "Rule of 72"

Just how big a problem can inflation be? Instead of producing charts with columns of numbers showing its negative impact, this might be a suitable place to introduce a handy "rule of thumb." Many of you will already be familiar with the "Rule of 72" which, simply put, says to divide the number 72 by the rate of inflation. The result will be the approximate number of years it will take for inflation to reduce your capital to *one half* its original value. For example, an inflation rate of six percent means $100,000 will be worth (in today's dollars) only $50,000 in 12 years (72 ÷ 6 = 12).

Or to offer a different scenario, an inflation rate of six percent will

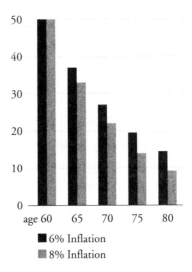

Inflation

The decling value of a
Fixed Income

Annual Income (000's)

■ 6% Inflation
■ 8% Inflation

reduce the purchasing power of a $50,000 a year income to only $25,000 a year in about 12 years (72÷6=12). This would mean that a person retiring at age 60 with enough capital to produce a $50,000 per year income would see that income's purchasing power fall to $25,000 by age 72 and to $12,500 by age 84 (which would be about normal life expectancy) *even if they were able to invest that capital at a rate equal to inflation!*

This is why we absolutely must look for investments which have traditionally beaten inflation.

Inflation, Volatility and Time Horizon

Here's where the crunch comes. *Investments that are most likely to outpace inflation over the long term are those with higher volatility!* So we have come full circle, back to the other major risk component – the "fluctuation factor." A well-structured investment portfolio has to account for the risk of both inflation and volatility. And, as noted previously, both are functions of time. In the short run, volatility is the greater hazard – our growth-type assets could be down in value at the very moment we want to "cash in." If, however, we have a reasonably long time horizon, then inflation becomes the greater risk, eroding accumulated wealth and eating away at the purchasing power of income. Thus, we must have growth assets in our portfolio. One of the keys to successful investing, therefore, must be to accurately determine how much time we really have and then to balance the risks of inflation and volatility.

Regrettably, in the past, most of us have severely misjudged our time horizon, thinking it to be much shorter than in fact it is. The consequence is that we have shied away from potentially volatile but inflation-beating assets in favour of lower-return, inflation-vulnerable ones. The general rule is that *long time horizon portfolios need inflation-fighting assets in them, while shorter time horizons require preservation of principal.*

It is at this point that I will diverge from what is the "conventional wisdom." Most of the commentary I've studied suggests that investors should significantly alter their investment portfolios when they retire to entirely eliminate assets which fluctuate in value. This implies, for example, that stocks should be traded in for GICs. In my opinion, that is wrong! In most cases, that is exactly what you should *not* do!

This erroneous conclusion comes about, I believe, because most advisors equate the end of an investor's time horizon with date of retirement. But unless you intend to be retired for only a short period of time, that may be the most colossal mistake you could make. In most cases, we are going to be retired as long as, or even longer, than we have been accumulating assets. Why, then, would we want to discard the only assets that have any chance of keeping pace with inflation over the 15 to 20 years most of us will be retired? If inflation was a concern when we were still receiving our cost-of-living adjusted incomes while working, it certainly will be a concern after that income stops. That's when we'll be trying to live on pension income, government benefits and whatever we can generate from our investment portfolio. If the first two are relatively fixed, the last one must be capable of outpacing inflation over the long term.

In most cases, a portfolio structured to accumulate wealth effectively between age 30 and 60 will also do the job of preserving that wealth and providing reasonable after-inflation income between age 60 and 90. Please bear with me on this. Later on we'll get to how to structure the portfolio so that your income from it doesn't fluctuate and the portfolio continues to grow. For now, however, please accept this: your time horizon is likely much longer than you thought and your portfolio will probably always need some equity-type assets.

Summary

- *There is no such thing as a risk-free investment!*
- *The challenge is to decide what* level of risk *you are willing to assume and then, having decided on your risk tolerance, to understand the* implications of that choice.
- *As investors, we are psychologically far more fragile than we thought. We now find more comfort in lower, predictable returns than in higher but more volatile ones.*
- *The two greatest risks investors face are* inflation *and* volatility.
- *Investments that are most likely to outpace inflation over the long term are those with higher volatility.*
- *Long time-horizon portfolios need inflation fighting assets in them, while shorter time horizons require preservation of principal.*
- *Most investors underestimate their time horizon by equating it with retirement.*

Chapter Three:

Saving, Loaning and Owning: The Basic Asset Classes

THERE IS A NATURAL ORDER TO THE BASIC ASSET CLASSES:
CASH – THE LEAST RISKY WITH THE LOWEST RETURNS;
DEBT – MODERATELY RISKY WITH MODERATE RETURNS; AND
EQUITIES – THE MOST RISKY BUT OFFERING THE GREATEST PAYOFF.

Several times up to this point we've mentioned things like "growth assets" or "interest-generating assets." It's time to be a little more specific and pick some examples of each which we can use throughout the balance of this book.

Essentially, there are only three basic classes of assets: cash, debt, and equity. Although there are literally thousands of investment alternatives, each asset can generally be placed in one of these three major categories.

Cash includes bank accounts, term deposits, money market mutual funds, Treasury Bills and other "short-term" instruments. Usually cashable on short notice, these should perhaps more accurately be called "savings" rather than investments. They typically earn interest (as compared to capital gains) and are generally perceived to be "low risk."

Debt comprises all contracts between a borrower and a lender, whether they are in writing or not, including bonds, debentures, mortgages and loans to your brother-in-law. These, too, typically earn interest. There is normally some "face value" associated with investments from this category which is collectible at the end of the contract period. For example, a $1,000 Canada Savings Bond, due in 1997, will be worth exactly $1,000 at maturity in 1997, excluding interest. The obvious exceptions are mortgages and outright loans which normally include some repayment of the original principal in every monthly cheque.

Because of the contractual nature of these investments, if you change your mind sometime during the term of the contract, there will usually be an adjustment in the "cash-in" value. This may increase or decrease the dollar amount you receive, depending on what has happened to interest rates since you made the investment. In general terms, if interest rates have gone up, you will normally be penalized in some way for breaking the contract, that is, cashing in early. Why? Because borrowers will presumably have to go out and replace the funds you lent them at a higher cost – higher interest charges – so you pay the difference. On the other hand, if rates have fallen, people borrowing money are usually happy to get out of the contract because they can probably replace your money with lower-cost funds, so they may even pay you a bonus! This is obviously a gross oversimplification, but it is sufficient for our purposes here. Thus, debt assets earn interest but also have capital gain or loss potential prior to maturity.

Equities are assets that increase or decrease in value (the fluctuation factor) depending on what someone is willing to pay for them at any particular moment. Common examples of equities are stocks, real estate, growth mutual funds, collectibles and private businesses. Although generally looked upon as investments which are expected to grow in value over time, they may also provide income. Stocks pay dividends, real estate generates rent and private businesses (hopefully!) issue regular paycheques to owner-employees. Of course, there are advantages and disadvantages to each asset class.

Cash-type vehicles offer liquidity. You can normally retrieve your money relatively painlessly. They offer a known rate of return, albeit only for a short time. If rates fall, you have to reinvest at the lower rates. On the other hand, if rates are rising, you can ride up with them because you don't have your money "locked in" for too long a period of time. The greatest risk with cash holdings is that, over the long term, they do not generate enough profit to offset inflation and allow the asset to grow in real purchasing power. From an investment perspective, cash assets' most useful feature is that they are readily available for opportunities or emergencies. Having cash in a portfolio also reduces its volatility (and correspondingly, its return).

The distinction between *debt*-type assets and cash assets is becoming increasingly blurry. As competition in the financial community heightens, investments are being offered that have much greater flexibility than they have had traditionally. You can now buy, for example, "cashable GICs" which permit you to opt out of the original contract before its expiry. The interest offered is lower, of course, than for a "non-cashable" product and, in fact, products such as these are really just the old bonus/discount practices described earlier marketed in a different way. However, debt assets have value in that, assuming they are kept to maturity, you'll know exactly how much they will be worth at that time.

On the down side, as discussed previously, these investments can fluctuate in value *during* the term. Furthermore, they have not done a very good job of keeping pace with inflation over the long term. I will illustrate this point more convincingly later.

This would probably be the appropriate place to comment on Canada Savings Bonds – the most popular investment choice of Canadians. In my opinion, Canada Savings Bonds should not be thought of as being in the same asset class as other bonds, that is, as debt. CSBs have a guaranteed interest rate for *one year only* and then an annually adjusted rate thereafter. For that reason alone, they should be regarded as cash-type investments or "savings," as the name implies.

Historically, the best returns – the ones most likely to provide a hedge against inflation – have come from *equities*. And so it must be, because these also entail the greatest amount of risk. The risk, of course, is the volatility – the "fluctuation factor" – in the short run. As I have stated already and will prove conclusively, the risk from volatility decreases over time, so the longer your time horizon, the better choice growth assets become.

The Natural Order

So here we have the three basic asset categories all neatly lined up in a row: cash – the least risky with the lowest returns; debt – moderately risky with moderate returns; and equities – the most risky but offering the greatest payoff. This is the natural order. It has to work out this way, even though it may occasionally get out of whack. *Over the long term*, the natural order will prevail. Why? Perhaps a simple example will illustrate the answer best.

Let us suppose that at the end of a month you found yourself with $100 left over. The pantry has been refilled, the bills paid, the new sweater purchased and enough restaurants visited. So you decide to "save" the extra $100. A good financial planner, by the way, would insist you save the hundred bucks first – otherwise there is seldom anything "left" at the end of the month. That's sound advice. However, for our purposes, let's just say you elect to put the money into your savings account at the bank.

The bank is going to pay you interest on your money because, in effect, you are lending it to them. The rate of interest won't be very high on a savings account because the bank doesn't know how long you intend to leave it there, so they have some restrictions on what they can do with your money. But let's say, for example, they pay you three percent interest. What, then, does the bank do with your money?

Well, one choice might be to lend it to someone else, perhaps, a business owner. Let's suppose they do that and they charge nine percent interest to borrow the money. What do business owners do with borrowed funds? Probably, they invest them in their own business. Why? Because they feel confident they can generate a return in excess of the nine percent it cost them to borrow the money. Otherwise, as good business people, they wouldn't do it.

So there is the natural order. You lend the bank your money for three percent; the bank lends the money to a business owner at nine percent; he or she invests it to earn, say 15 percent. The return obviously increases as the risk does. There is little chance that the bank won't have your $100 when you go to claim it so the interest they pay you has little or no allowance for risk. There is some chance, however, that the business owner may default on the loan so bankers demand a premium in the form of higher interest charges to compensate them for that possibility. From the perspective of business owners, if they are going to invest in their own firm, with all the risks that assumes, they have to expect a higher reward than if they had simply left their money in the bank.

As investors, we have the opportunity to place our money in any of the three basic asset categories. We can leave it in cash, that is, put it in the bank. That would, in this example, earn us three percent. Another option might be to buy a Treasury Bill for a slightly higher return. We could lend it directly to someone through a loan or mortgage or to the government by purchasing a bond. We would hope to earn about nine percent in that case. Alternatively, we could invest directly into a business enterprise by purchasing shares of that firm on the stock market. In this example, like the business owner, we would want to earn something in the neighbourhood of 15 percent for doing that. The choice becomes the level of risk we are willing to assume, based on the rate of return we expect to receive.

Basic Asset Classes Risks and Advantages

Asset Class	Risk	Advantage
Cash	Long run inflation	Liquidity
Debt	Mid-term volatility/long run inflation	Fixed maturity value
Equity	Short-term volatility	Inflation hedge

Rates of Return

The final step in preparing ourselves psychologically to invest is to develop some realistic expectations about the kind of returns we are likely to achieve by choosing among the three basic asset classes. To simplify the whole process, I am going to pick just one specific investment from each class and use it as a representative for the entire class. Again, this will not give us 100 percent accuracy, but it will illustrate the notion of asset allocation reasonably well. You can substitute your own investment preferences for the ones I have chosen. It is the *concept* that is most important at this stage.

As the saying goes, "History has a way of repeating itself" so we'll begin with a review of how these asset classes have performed in the past. We will then project the current trends into the future. The most likely candidates for examples are those for which we can obtain the most data – this will aid our accuracy. With that in mind, I have chosen the following:

Asset Class	Investment
Cash	Treasury Bills
Debt	Government Bonds
Equities	Stocks

More specifically, we will use Government of Canada 91 Day Treasury Bills for our cash component; Government of Canada Bonds with maturities in excess of 10 years to represent the debt portion; and the Toronto Stock Exchange (TSE) Index for stock price change calculations. The Consumer Price Index (CPI) will reflect changes in the cost of living.

Don't be alarmed! Even I don't want to spend too much time making complicated calculations on the return differentials among these assets. The data we need is well developed in a publication titled *Canadian Stocks, Bonds, Bills, and Inflation: 1950-1987* by James E. Hatch and Robert W. White, published by The Research Foundation of the Institute of Chartered Financial Analysts. Our numbers are derived from their research. We will be examining the forty-three year period from 1951 through 1993 and I have, therefore, added six more years data to the 1950-1987 tabulations by Mr. Hatch and Mr. White.

Summary

- *The three basic asset classes are cash, debt and equities.*
- *There is a* natural order *to the basic asset classes:*
  Cash - the least risky with the lowest returns;
  Debt - moderately risky with moderate returns; and
  Equities - the most risky but offering the greatest payoff.

Chapter Four:

Do You Believe in Magic?

MOST INVESTORS HAVE PORTFOLIOS THAT ARE TOO
SMALL TO MEET ALL THEIR OBJECTIVES,
GIVEN REALISTIC EXPECTATIONS FOR RETURN.

Investment Performance

Investment advisors tell me repeatedly that the greatest challenge they face is trying to develop, in the minds of their clients, realistic expectations about rates of return. Most of us are far too optimistic.

The delusion appears to have emerged from the fact that, as suggested earlier, our investment decision-making is shaped by outside influences and past experiences. We believe that higher returns are possible with less risk than is really the case. And why not? If we have not personally a) had a stock double in price; b) earned 20 percent on bonds; c) gotten 14 percent on T-Bills; or d) watched our real estate holdings soar in value, then we probably know someone who has!

However, our memories get a little clouded from time to time. Occasionally, we conveniently forget that real estate and stocks go down in value and that people trying to live on interest from their bond portfolios shudder every time rates fall. Amazing isn't it, the way we protect ourselves from painful memories? And as we discovered during these unsettling periods, we are not as stalwart as we thought. We want some security in our investments, some constant. Thus we are now willing to accept lower, stable returns over higher but more volatile ones. At the same time, we are beginning to understand the need for *compromise*. We are coming to the realization that stable and predictable means lower returns while higher, long-term growth is achieved only with some volatility along the way.

So how do we meld these apparently conflicting ideals and desires into some sort of investment philosophy? Unquestionably, it is something we must do. Why? Because the whole purpose of investing is to meet some sort of financial objective. Regrettably, as most financial planners know, most people have portfolios which are too small to meet all their objectives, given realistic expectations for return. Yet because we continue to think in terms of 20 percent bond yields and the 30 percent mutual funds have earned from time to time, we believe all things are possible. What we need are some reasonable and realistic expectations about investment returns. Only then can we approach the task of setting achievable goals for our portfolios with confidence.

Realistic Expectations — Realistic Objectives

Annual Returns

Here is where I let the economist in me out to play. Economists love graphs and charts like the ones that follow. Unfortunately, most non-economists find them boring, so let's get through them as quickly as possible. These are essentially the same graphs we looked at previously, but our examination will now be a little more specific.

The first one shows the actual results on a year-by-year basis for Treasury Bills and Government of Canada Bonds and the Consumer Price Index (CPI) for the period 1951-1993. What do we see? Well, first of all, each line fluctuates - some more than others. We knew that was going to happen. The T-Bill line and the CPI line tend to move pretty much in parallel while the bond results are more varied, again, more or less as anticipated, given our previous discussion about cash and debt instruments. The important thing to note, however, is the *range* within which these three lines fluctuate. As was pointed out before, interest rate fluctuations have become wider over the past few years. There are also several periods when the inflation line is higher than the bond and T-Bill line.

Annual Price Changes (1951-1993)

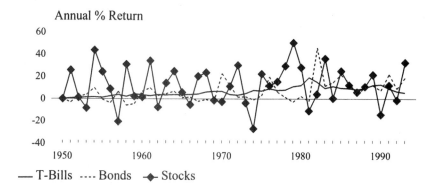

— T-Bills ···· Bonds — ··· CPI

Okay, that takes care of two of the three asset classes. Let's add the third one: stocks.

Annual Price Changes (1951-1993)

— T-Bills ···· Bonds ◆ Stocks

Look at the difference! See how erratic the stock results have been and how much wider the range is. Given that kind of volatility, why would anyone invest in the stock market? The answer can be found in the next graph.

Cumulative Return (1951-1993)

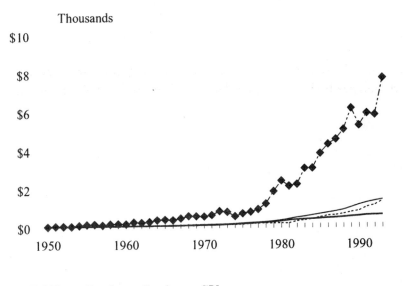

— T-Bills ··· Bonds ◆ Stocks — CPI

If we "stretch out" the lines by adding all the positive results together and subtracting any negative ones, we are left with the cumulative trend lines indicated. The significance is apparent from the dollar figures shown. Recall the $100 we put in the bank a few pages ago? If we had, in fact, invested that $100 in bonds back in 1951 and re-invested all interest earned, we would have had $1401 by the end of 1993. Similarly, $100 used to buy a T-Bill would have grown slightly more, to $1482. But investing that $100 in the stock market would have us owning a portfolio worth almost $7660 — that's five or six better than the alternatives!

So why wouldn't we put all of our money in the stock market? Take a look back at the lower graph on page 43 — it would be just too darned painful! The volatility of the stock market would leave most of us bleary-eyed from sleepless nights. In the 43 year period between 1951 and 1993, there have been at least 10 significant market declines. How many of us would have been strong enough to have held on through those downturns? If the stock market had been our only investment choice, depending on when we started and stopped, we could either be very rich or very poor. Because in that same 43 year span, the stock market has also gone up substantially at least 10 times! But because the markets have, on a cumulative basis, risen more than they have declined, stock investors who had a long enough time horizon always came out ahead of bond and T-Bill investors.

These previous graphs have all shown what is referred to as nominal return, that is, before inflation. If we adjust the numbers by subtracting annual increases in the cost of living, the *real* results are $720 for bonds, $801 for Treasury Bills and a whopping $6981 for stocks. That means that over a 43 year period, we gained a total of $620 on our original $100 (about 4.7% per year) by buying bonds or $701 on our T-Bill account (about 5% per year). Our stock portfolio, on the other hand, increased in value by $7560 or an average of 10.6 percent per year. Again, a startling advantage for stocks over the other two choices.

Range of Results

It's time to bring out some of "the big guns" to prove without a doubt what I have been saying about the relative attractiveness of T-Bills, bonds and stocks as investment alternatives. The following table is intimidating in appearance simply because of the amount of data it presents. Study it if you wish. Otherwise skip to the shorter summary titled "Stocks and The Importance of Time." It has most of the good stuff in it anyway.

Investment Results – Various Time Horizons

	Stocks	Bonds	T-Bills	CPI
43 One-Year Time Horizons				
Highest Annual % Return	51.3%	45.87%	19.1%	12.3%
Lowest Annual % Return	-28.3%	-5.8%	0.5%	-1.7%
# Periods w/Negative Return	11	12	0	2
# Periods Outpacing Inflation	30	23	32	n/a
# Periods w/Best Return	20/43	13/43	10/43	n/a
	(46%)	(30%)	(24%)	

	Stocks	Bonds	T-Bills	CPI
39 Five-Year Time Horizons				
Highest Annual % Return	26.3%	22.6%	13.4%	10.2%
Lowest Annual % Return	-0.2%	-1.6%	1.1%	0.4%
# Periods w/Negative Return	1	2	0	0
# Periods Outpacing Inflation	33	23	32	n/a
# Periods w/Best Return	25/39	8/39	7/39	n/a
	(64%)	(21%)	(15%)	

	Stocks	Bonds	T-Bills	CPI
34 Ten-Year Time Horizons				
Highest Annual % Return	17.7%	17.2%	11.3%	9.7%
Lowest Annual % Return	3.8%	0.4%	2.0%	1.0%
# Periods w/Negative Return	0	0	0	0
# Periods Outpacing Inflation	33	21	27	n/a
# Periods w/Best Return	26/34	5/34	3/34	n/a
	(77%)	(15%)	(8%)	

Investment Results – Various Time Horizons (cont)

	Stocks	Bonds	T-Bills	CPI
19 25-Year Time Horizons				
Highest Annual % Return	11.9%	10.2%	9.1%	6.5%
Lowest Annual % Return	6.7%	2.7%	3.6%	3.0%
# Periods w/Negative Return	0	0	0	0
# Periods Outpacing Inflation	19	12	19	n/a
# Periods w/Best Return	19/19	0/19	0/19	n/a
	(100%)	(0%)	(0%)	

Here are the summary numbers that I find so very convincing:

Stocks and the Importance of Time (1951-1993)

	Time Horizon			
	1 Yr.	5 Yr.	10 Yr.	25 Yr.
	(43)	(39)	(34)	(19)
Stock Results				
Highest Annual % Return	51.3%	26.3%	17.7%	11.9%
Lowest Annual % Return	-28.3%	-0.2%	3.8%	6.7%
# Periods w/Negative Return	11	1	0	0
# Periods Outpacing Inflation	29	33	33	19
# Periods w/Best Return	20/43	25/39	26/34	19/19
	(46%)	(64%)	(77%)	(100%)

Time Horizon – The Key

The value in these statistics is their ability to point out the importance of time horizon when considering stock investments. In the 43 years between 1951 and 1993, there were, obviously, 43 one-year investment periods. Under the first column, then, are the results assuming investments were held for one year only. We see that the highest annual return in that 43 year period was 51.3 percent and the lowest in any one year was -28.3 percent. That's quite a range!

Looking further down that same column, stocks had negative returns 11 out of the 43 years. On a more optimistic note, a stock portfolio would have beaten inflation 30 of the 43 one-year periods. Finally, stocks provided the best returns (compared to T-Bills and bonds) 46 percent of the time, that is 20 out of 43 years.

Let's expand the time horizon now to five years. In the period intervening 1951 and 1993, there were 39 opportunities to invest for five years (1951-1955, 1952-1956,...1989-1993.) What happens when we extend our holdings to five years?

As indicated in the second column, the highest average annual return over five years dropped to 26.3 percent and the lowest average annual return climbed substantially (although still negative) to -0.2 percent. So whereas the range of results over one-year periods was almost 80 percent (-28.3% up to +51.3%), when we stretch our holding to five years, that range narrows by about two-thirds to about 26 percent (-0.2% up to +26.3%).

Examining the rest of that column shows us that we would have had positive returns in all but one of the five-year periods and would have beaten inflation 33 out of 39 times. Stock outperformed T-Bills and bonds almost two out of three times.

I won't summarize the other columns for 10-year and 25-year holding periods. You can do that yourself. It is sufficient to say that as the time horizon is expanded, stocks become increasingly better investments: the volatility declines and they are the best for keeping up with increases in the cost of living. This is why I am so adamant that people who are retiring, in good health at, say, age 60 or 65 should not suddenly dispose of all their equity-type investments.

These tables also provide irrefutable proof that over the long term, stocks outperform bonds and T-Bills. The all-important element, though, is time. Our conclusion from this can only be that *portfolios with long time horizons need equities to offset inflation while shorter time frames require debt and/or cash investments to reduce volatility.*

Summary

- *Most of us are far too optimistic about the rates of return we can potentially earn on various investments over the long term.*
- *Most investors have portfolios which are too small to meet all their objectives, given realistic expectations for return.*
- *We are coming to the realization that stable and predictable means lower returns while higher, long-term growth is achieved only with some volatility along the way.*
- *Over the long term, equities outperform debt and cash-type investments.*
- *Portfolios with long time horizons need equities to offset inflation while shorter time frames require debt and/or cash investments to reduce volatility.*

Chapter Five:

Realistic
Expectations

WHILE EQUITY MARKETS WILL FLUCTUATE, OVER TIME,
THE OVERALL DIRECTION WILL BE UP.

Future Returns

So much for the past. Where do we go from here? What can we realistically expect to happen with rates of return from this point forward?

I was in the audience at a conference of the International Association for Financial Planning in New Orleans when the guest speaker, Louis Rukeyzer, the congenial host of *Wall Street Week,* was asked to predict the future of the stock market. His answer? "It will fluctuate." And world-renowned economist Milton Freidman, when asked the same question, replied, "The only thing I know about the market is that it will fluctuate." And so it will. If there is anything we have learned over the past 100 years or so of investing, it is that returns will vary from good to not-so-good. However, there are a couple of trends, already developed in the preceding pages, on which we can rely.

First, while stock markets will fluctuate, over time, the overall direction will be up. Over what period of time? Clearly, from the previous data, a time horizon of ten years would not be unreasonable.

Secondly, stocks, again over time, will outperform cash or bonds. By how much? That is the question we are going to address now. And here is some advance notice of the answer: not by much, but by enough to make a huge difference in a long-term investment program.

Determining Rates of Return

Let's look first at how rates of return are derived. We alluded to this in our earlier discussion of the $100 investment. So for simplicity, let's stick with that example.

The rate of return I should realistically expect to earn on any investment is a function of three components:

1. Riskless real return,
2. Inflation factor and
3. Risk premium(s).

That is, if I am to invest my $100, I should expect to be rewarded in some way for the use of my money, for decreases in purchasing power between the time I invest it and the time it is returned to me and for any chance that I won't get my money back or that it will have declined in value while invested.

In Canada, our experience is that a real rate of return of about two percent is satisfying enough for the use of our money. Two percent! "Not me!", you say. Doesn't sound like much, does it? But hang on a minute… to that we would have to add an allowance for inflation. So in our very simple example, if I put my $100 into a so-called "risk-free" investment such as a Canada Savings Bond for a one year period and I expect inflation to be about six per cent during that interval, I should realistically expect to earn eight percent on that investment (2% real return + 6% inflation factor). So my $100 bond should be worth $108 by the end of the first year.

Of course, we all know now that there really is no such thing as a truly "risk-free" investment because of the inflation phenomenon. However, since we've accounted for declining purchasing power with our inflation factor allowance, I guess it's okay to assume the government won't default on its obligations and we also know that CSBs are normally held for more than one year, but this will serve as a reasonable example. Here's what it looks like in tabular form:

Example #1

Riskless Real Return	2%
Inflation	6%
Risk (Canada Savings Bond)	0%
Total Expected Return	*8%*

How would it work out for riskier investments, say, pork belly futures? Something like this:

Example #2

Riskless Real Return	2%
Inflation	6%
Risk Commodities	20%
Total Expected Return	*28%*

So I should not invest my hundred bucks in pork bellies unless I am reasonably confident of having it grow to be worth $128 in an acceptable period of time. And so it is with any investment alternative you may choose. The reward has to bear some relationship to the anticipated risk.

Let's get back to our three basic asset examples. How do they stack up in this equation? From that large data table shown before, we can summarize the actual range of results in Canada over the past 43 years as follows:

Range of Annual Returns

	Low	High
Treasury Bills	+0.5%	+19.9%
Bonds	-5.8%	+45.3%
Stocks	-28.3%	+51.3%
Inflation	-1.7%	+12.3%

Expected Returns and Expected Risk

Well having a range of returns is nice, you say, but how does that help me determine what I can realistically expect from my portfolio now and over my personal time horizon? Do I simply expect my stocks, for example, to fluctuate between -28 percent and +51 percent? No, that wouldn't be very useful. Even in our quest to be only approximately right, we do want some measure of precision. The mathematicians among us will quickly say something like, "Yes, there is significant *standard deviation* here, but in fact the results are, more or less, *normally distributed* about a *mean*."

Huh? Translation: Despite the wide range of results, there are some *averages* that are fairly accurate and predictable. We can use them to estimate expected rates of return.

Furthermore, the mathematicians would want to talk about arithmetic and geometric means. Let's just call them "averages" and trust that I've chosen the correct one for our purposes. And of course, the number cruncher would certainly want to explore *variance* and *standard deviation* in more detail. I prefer our earlier terminology: the "fluctuation factor" or volatility. So let's try to put all this together — in English!

From our research we have determined that the three assets we have chosen along with inflation have, over the past 43 years, shown the following *average* results:

Asset	Compound Annual Return	Fluctuation
T-Bills	6%	± 4%
Bonds	6%	±10%
Stocks	11%	±18%
Inflation	5%	± 4%

That means, for example, that Treasury Bills have averaged six percent per year over that period but have normally fluctuated between two percent (6% - 4%) and 10 percent (6% + 4%). Stocks have ranged from negative seven percent (11% - 18%) to positive 29 percent (11% + 18%), averaging 11 percent. Now we know from the previous data that, in fact, the actual spread between the highest and lowest results was much greater. What we are illustrating here is the "normal" range of results.

Perhaps an analogy might help make this more clear. Think of the weather, specifically the temperature. For any particular day of the year, there is a "normal high" and "normal low" temperature for your locale. You hear it referred to every morning on the radio. What the weather forecasters are saying, of course, is that for that time of the year they "expect" temperatures to fall within a certain range. We also know, only too well sometimes, that they are not always right! That bright, sunny day on which they convince us to leave home without a jacket is often the one that suddenly turns cool and leaves us shivering all the way home.

If you happen to be a golf nut like I am, you might prefer an example using golf scores and handicaps. If you are a "scratch" golfer, you would normally expect to shoot around 72 – the normal par for a championship course. But your experience tells you that your score varies from round to round, say, from 68 to 75 – but still with an average of 72. A 10 handicap golfer would expect to score about 82 but the range would likely be between, say, 78 and 89. Occasionally, of course, we all have some exceptional games – with scores that we rush home to tell ignored spouses about — and others where our only comments are that the group ahead of us was playing too slowly.

Well so it is with investment returns. We "expect" them to fall within a certain range. But occasionally, unpredictably and for reasons that we can only explain afterwards, they are higher or lower. That's what the mathematician means when he refers to "standard deviation"; there is about a *two out of three chance* that returns will be as anticipated. The other one-third of the time, they will be greater or less than expected.

Today's Expected Returns

The averages in the previous chart are compiled from the results of the past 43 years. However, as seen already, the range of investment returns has been expanding in more recent times. In most cases, they have been going up. For example, in the 1950s, Treasury Bills earned a maximum of four percent; through the 1960s, the highest rate was about seven percent; by the end of the next decade, it had reached over 11 percent. In 1981, rates peaked at 19 percent and have been more or less declining since then. As I am writing this, T-Bill rates have fallen to less than five percent and are expected to continue even lower.

With this trend and the respective ones for bonds and stocks in mind, I have boldly set out the following as the averages we will use in designing our portfolios for the next few years. Keep in mind that these are *averages;* we expect that about two out of three times, returns will fall within these ranges. There will certainly, however, be years when we will be way off, but trust me, in the long run, it really won't matter very much that one, two, three, four or even five years were above or below the expected averages. It is worth repeating: "it is better to be *approximately right rather than precisely wrong.*"

Here, then, are my numbers:

Asset	Compound Annual Return	Fluctuation
T-Bills	7%	±4%
Bonds	8%	±10%
Stocks	12%	±18%
Inflation	5%	±4%

Taxes

In the introduction of this book, I stated that we were not going to spend much time on the taxation of various investment alternatives because that was a broad enough topic in itself and I am not a tax expert. Having said that, however, it is appropriate here to make just a couple of comments.

The Canadian tax system encourages us to choose one investment vehicle over another by giving us preferential treatment for certain types of income. Interest earned, for example, on a term deposit, is taxable at full personal rates whereas dividends are taxed, through a tax credit arrangement, at a much lower rate. Another advantageous investment from a tax viewpoint is one that generates a capital gain, because under current legislation, even though the first $100,000 is no longer exempt from tax, only 75 percent of capital gains are taxable.

This is a very simplistic explanation and implies that one should only invest in dividend-generating assets. Indeed, if minimizing taxes were the only consideration, that might well be the best route. However, as has already been expressed several times, there are many things to weigh in choosing appropriate investments. I will explore taxation a little further when we come to actually implementing the strategies developed over the next few chapters. For now, my advice is to get yourself one of the many good books on tax or consult an expert.

Summary

- *While equity markets will fluctuate, over time, the overall direction will be up.*
- *Rates of return are a function of three components:*
  1. Riskless real return,
  2. Inflation factor and
  3. Risk premium(s)
- *Over the past 43 years, the* average *experience has been:*

Asset	Compound Annual Return	Fluctuation
T-Bills	6%	±4%
Bonds	6%	±10%
Stocks	11%	±18%
Inflation	5%	±4%

- *The Canadian tax system encourages us to choose one investment vehicle over another by giving us preferential treatment for certain types of income.*

Upward and Onward

So Part I of our task is completed. Preparing ourselves psychologically to invest is a critical and crucial first step. It establishes a solid foundation on which we can rely as we put together our strategies and actually implement them. Let's review what has been accomplished. So far, we have:

- *Discovered that, as investors, we are subject to* human frailties. *We often make irrational decisions even when we know better. There is hope, however. Recognizing the weaknesses of human nature goes a long way towards minimizing the damage they can cause.*
- *Accepted that the real choice is not to find a risk-free investment, but to decide what* level of risk *we are willing to assume and then to understand the implications of that choice.*
- *Learned that* inflation *is an insidious "double demon" that depletes accumulated capital and reduces the purchasing power of income.*
- *Recognized that* volatility *is a greater hazard than inflation in the short run. Over the long term, however, assets with higher volatility are more likely to outpace inflation than assets with low volatility are.*
- *Sorted investment alternatives into three basic asset classes:* cash, debt *and* equities. *These can respectively be represented by Treasury Bills, bonds and stocks – each with advantages and disadvantages.*
- *Concluded that equities outperform all other investments over the long term. Therefore, portfolios with long time horizons need equities to offset the inflation risk. However, most people* underestimate time horizon *because they equate it with retirement.*

Inflation continues after retirement, thus most investors should not dramatically alter their portfolios at that time.

• *Realized that most of us tend to be overly optimistic. We believe higher returns are possible with less risk than is really the case. Most investors, however, need some constant and, recognizing the* need *for* compromise, *will accept lower, stable returns over higher, more volatile ones.*

• *Proved that returns for the various asset classes fall within certain ranges. Although the year-by-year results may vary substantially, the* long-term averages are quite predictable *as is the extent to which the returns will normally vary.*

• *Estimated, using reasonable assumptions,* realistic expected rates of return *for the three asset classes over the next few years.*

Let us now move on to Part II – spelling out a personal invest-ment philosophy and setting achievable investment objectives.

Chapter Six:

Developing Your Investment Philosophy

A RATIONAL INVESTOR WILL TAKE ON GREATER RISK IF THE
ANTICIPATED REWARD IS SUFFICIENT.

Risk Tolerance + Personality = Philosophy

So now we have a strong conceptual base from which to build a successful investment strategy. With the foundation laid as to why and how we generally make investment decisions, it is time to become more specific and get down to the real world as it applies to a population of one: you! We now have to zero in on what makes up *your* personal investment *philosophy.*

We'll do this in two stages. First, let's go back to something we discussed at length already – *risk tolerance.* Now I want to lead you through a couple of exercises to help you more accurately determine your personal risk profile. We've talked a lot about risk and have come to understand its characteristics and impact. As noted, our observations so far have been about investors in general. But how do you, as an individual, react to risk?

Secondly, we want to get a handle on your investment *personality.* It is as unique as all other parts of your personality. To a certain extent, your behaviour as an investor is a function of your risk tolerance. But there are other considerations.

Arising out of these exercises, then, will be a composite picture of you, the investor. With that in hand, we can set about designing an investment portfolio appropriate for your individual philosophy.

Risk Tolerance

You know from your own experience and observation that some people are willing to take more risk than others. Certain brave souls will sky dive, race motorcycles and climb sheer rock faces. The physical risks, in their minds, are worth the psychological rewards for having challenged themselves.

In investing, as we have already established, a rational investor will take on greater risk if the anticipated reward is sufficient. But just as the adventurers described above wouldn't jump out of airplanes, roar around a race course or scale a cliff without careful planning and the proper equipment, intelligent investors won't expose themselves to undue risk.

What if I were to offer you a potential return of, say, 50 percent on a highly speculative investment? In all likelihood, you would turn me down if you thought there was a reasonable chance you would lose all or even part of your money. Similarly, if I presented an opportunity to earn only two per cent but with minimal risk, you would probably decline that offer as well, assured that you could do better elsewhere. It would be fair to say, then, that somewhere between investments that potentially earn 50 percent but with high risk exposure and those that pay only two per cent but don't pose much risk is your "comfort zone."

Realistically, in fact, the range is likely to be much narrower than from two percent to 50 percent. Just how large is your comfort zone and how can we be more accurate about the types of investments that will fit into it?

Perhaps one way to focus in on the breadth of returns you find acceptable would be to examine how you already have your assets invested. Take a couple of minutes to complete this simple chart. Don't worry about being too precise. Round off the dollar values. This is just to get a quick "feel" for where you are today.

Lower Risk		Moderate Risk		Higher Risk	
Personal Dwelling	$_____	Bonds	$_____	Stocks	$_____
Bank Accounts	$_____	Loans	$_____	Collectibles	$_____
Term Deposits	$_____	Rental Property	$_____	Tax Shelters	$_____
Other(s)	$_____	Other(s)	$_____	Other(s)	$_____
	$_____		$_____		$_____
	$_____		$_____		$_____
Total	$_____	Total	$_____	Total	$_____
Grand Total	$_____				
Lower Risk %	_____	Moderate Risk %	_____	Higher Risk %	_____

Some readers may want to argue that certain assets are in the wrong columns. That's okay. Move them around if you wish. *Perception* of risk is almost as important as the level of risk itself. We are defining *your* comfort zone, so make this exercise meaningful for you.

I suspect, however, that most readers will find themselves very heavily weighted towards the left side of the page. Don't fret if you think, as a result of our previous comments, that you should have greater diversification of risk. Most Canadians are relatively low-risk investors. That's our nature, remember? And besides, this is just an attempt to develop a general idea of how you like to invest. I do caution you, however, to give some thought to how you came to owning the assets you have. Is most of your money invested in CSBs, for example, because you feel they are the best place to be or simply because they were "convenient" or the investments with which you were most familiar? In other words, are the assets you own today there by default or as a result of good planning?

Here is the second simple exercise to help get a handle on your risk tolerance. Imagine for a moment that all of your assets have been converted to cash; you've sold everything you owned and what you have in its place is a pile of dollar bills. Obviously, the larger your asset base to begin with, the greater number of dollars you will have. It doesn't matter; the concept will hold for any amount. Now imagine that you live in a world where you have only *two* investment choices: you can buy a T-Bill or invest in the stock market. Those are the only options available but you can split the money between them if you wish.

Remember from Chapter 4 that T-Bills will earn an average of seven percent interest with a fluctuation factor of ±4 percent, so from three percent to 11 percent. Investing in the stock market, on the other hand, should yield about 12 percent on average but will fluctuate between -6 percent and +30 percent. Given these assumptions, how would you allocate the money?

T - Bills _____% Stocks _____%

If you would leave everything in T-Bills (cash), you are best described not as an investor but as a *saver*. On the other hand, if you would place the full amount in the stock market (equities), some might even call you a gambler. Most people are not at either extreme and would fall somewhere in between, choosing to allocate a portion of their money to each of the two options.

Although this is far from precise, we might use the following broad asset allocations to describe risk tolerance in general terms:

% Cash	% Stocks	Risk Tolerance
100	0	Very Low
75	25	Low
50	50	Moderate
25	75	High
0	100	Very High

There are, by the way, a number of detailed questionnaires and even computer programs that can be used to try to pinpoint your risk tolerance. Personally, I don't believe the results of these are much more accurate than those you'll get with these two simple exercises. However, if you would like to have what you probably already know confirmed by someone else, please feel free to do so.

It is also important to keep in mind that your risk profile can change as your personal situation does, as your responsibilities and liabilities increase or lessen or as experiences shape your attitudes. All you can do is make the best decisions you can, based on the way you feel today. If your tolerance for risk changes at some point in the future, you will have to re-evaluate earlier choices to determine if they are still appropriate. As we proceed, I will be providing you with some guidelines for ongoing review and making changes to your investment strategy. For now, however, in general terms, how would you describe your risk tolerance: high, low, moderate?

Your Investment Personality

It's time now to explore the second aspect of your investment philosophy – that is, your investment *personality*. Again, bear in mind that the way you think, feel and behave as an investor is shaped to a certain extent by your risk tolerance but there is more to it than that.

I have derived a very simple method for assessing investment personality. And like most overly simplified things, this won't give us perfect accuracy but my experience is that it will be reasonably indicative. To follow this exercise through, all you have to do is to position yourself somewhere along *two* lines which describe different dimensions of personality. I've named the two lines *Involvement* and *Spontaneity*. Let's look at them one at a time.

Involvement

As the word implies, what we are trying to determine with this measurement is the degree to which you want to be involved in day-to-day investment decision-making. The basic question is "Are you an *active* or a *passive* investor?" Do you want to be very involved or are you the type who likes to leave those details to others? Let's consider some extreme examples.

Very *active* investors are the ones who say or think things like, "If an investment catches my eye, it doesn't take long for me to decide to jump in." These people like to be where the action is. They are afraid of being left out and are always asking, "Gee, should I be in *this* or *that?*" Active investors tend to have shorter time perspectives and seek chances to cash in on current trends and the "investment du jour."

At the other end of the spectrum, very *passive* investors really don't want to be involved very much at all in the decision-making process. They tend to let other people tell them what is best. In fact, they rely a great deal on the advice of others. They trust their advisors, often to a fault, but once a good relationship is established, they are very loyal. The most extreme passive investor would be one who says, "Here's all my money. Please call me when I'm rich!"

Most investors, of course, fall somewhere between the two extremes. Make an initial attempt to plot yourself on the Involvement line. Do you fall closer to the active or the passive end? Know that there is no good or bad place to be: successful investor personalities can be found all along the continuum.

Involvement

Spontaneity

The second dimension on which I'd like you to rank yourself is spontaneity. This one may require a little more explanation because, unlike the active/passive notion which is familiar to many activities, the spon-

70

taneity theory involves a couple of investment concepts that need to be developed first. They are "market timing" and "money management." Even if you have not run across these terms specifically before, you can probably guess what they mean.

Market Timing

Market timers are normally confident investors and make statements like, "I prefer opportunities with potentially large returns even if they are a little more risky." They are often entrepreneurial and strong-willed, finding a well diversified approach to investing to be somewhat boring. Most telling, as the term implies, market timers attempt to predict in which way and when investment markets will move. They then re-position their assets to take advantage of the anticipated change. So you will hear statements from experienced market timers such as, "Now is the time to invest in international stocks because the Canadian dollar is so strong that, at some point in the near future, it has to go the other way." The most frequent use of this tactic, however, is in timing stock and bond market fluctuations, so let's look at an example of each.

Market timers who believe the stock market is set for a decline will sell all the shares they own and place the proceeds into bonds and/or Treasury Bills. In this manner, they avoid losses. When they feel the market has bottomed, they will repurchase the then lower-cost stocks to take advantage of the expected upturn in prices.

The same tactic could work for interest-generating instruments. A market timer who feels that interest rates are going to fall will buy, for example, long term bonds to "lock in" the highest rates. The timer will also hope, in this example, to profit from increases in long-term bond prices which come about when interest rates fall. Subsequently, when those rates appear poised for an upward rebound, successful market timers will purchase short-term instruments so they can "ride up" with the escalating interest returns.

In theory, the true market timer will be fully invested in only one asset class a time. After all, if you believe that T-Bills will return more than stocks, why keep any money in the stock market? Because as a market timer, you are also saying that you can tell when that situation will reverse itself. Then you will move back into equities. The shifts among asset classes which a market timer will make are usually triggered by some sort of technical evaluation, such as the yield differential between stocks and bonds or something like the price patterns of a 39-day moving average for the Dow Jones or TSE indices. Indeed, there are some very sophisticated computer programs and advisory services which purport to be very successful at market timing.

Money Management

Fully disciplined money managers, on the other hand, do not believe that market timing works. Their strategy is to diversify an investment portfolio among the three major asset classes of cash, debt and equities in accordance with an investor's risk profile (much like we did when I asked you to imagine that you had only two ways to invest your money). The rationale for doing so is that diversification will reduce overall risk because it is unlikely that, for example, stocks and bonds will both fall in value at the same instant (although it does occasionally occur for short periods of time). Including cash-type assets which, theoretically, cannot decline in value, puts a "floor" under the portfolio to stabilize it. A portfolio diversified among cash, bonds and stocks will have less fluctuation than a pure equity one.

The money management approach also enables investors to satisfy their individual preferences by "fine tuning" their portfolios. This is accomplished by shifting the weightings of the assets held – for example, holding more equities if the investor wants an aggressive stance or fewer if the investor is more conservative. Typically, money management requires a longer-term perspective on investment results. Money management types are also often strong willed, but not rash. They are thoughtful persons by nature, frequently doing their own research and usually seeking to avoid volatility.

My Own View

I confess to favoring the money management approach, as perhaps you might have guessed. And the primary reason is because it accounts for the risk tolerance of the investor. The market timing tactic simply attempts to maximize return without regard for the psychological battering that transferring in and out of the various asset classes inflicts on the investor. In fairness, some investors "savour the action." I don't.

Secondly, the research I have conducted has failed to convince me that market timing yields any better results over the long term than a simple "buy and hold" strategy. Recall, for example, the graph of stock prices from earlier chapters which showed that there have been 10 significant stock market declines over the past forty years. Correspondingly, of course, there have been 10 major rises. This means that market timers would have had 20 opportunities to guess right... or wrong, because to be truly effective, they have to get it right twice each time – once getting out of the market and again getting back in. That seems like an incredible challenge to me and although some professionals insist they don't have to be correct more than half the time to make a difference, I'm not totally convinced of the merit of pure market timing.

There is overwhelming evidence in favour of the money management approach. For example, a recent survey of large pension plans in the United States proved conclusively that over 90 percent of a portfolio's investment result was determined by the asset allocation – that is, by what percentage of the portfolio was invested in cash, debt or equities. Less than three percent of the performance could be attributed to market timing and, in some cases, the impact of timing attempts was actually negative.

Furthermore, in Canada the average "bull" stock market lasts about 33 months – but 60 percent of the market's gain occurs, on average, in the first seven months. The key to success under those conditions, therefore, is clearly to be *in* the market *not out* of it. And we haven't even considered transaction costs or taxation. It is expensive to buy and sell assets frequently and taxes are often triggered which might otherwise be deferred.

Is There Any Place for Market Timing?

After reading this diatribe against market timing, you must be asking yourself, "Is there any place for it at all?" Yes, there is. Like most investment strategies, market timing can be practiced in degrees, and in fairness, what I have just described as market timing is an extreme. It is often referred to as "tactical" market timing. In fact, somewhere between tactical market timing and equally purist fundamental money management lies a "strategic" position that would likely serve investors well. That strategy might better be called "timing the market" than "market timing" and this is not a game of semantics. Clearly, if you as an investor are confident from your own intuition, experience, research or the advice of others that a long-term trend is emerging within a particular asset class, you can do your own "fine tuning" by shifting the weightings in your portfolio. However, you'll want to be able to make the adjustments easily and inexpensively and be conscious of the risk. Inevitably, the trend will reverse itself, so plan your escape too! If you are going to attempt market timing, perhaps you would be best to look upon it as a defensive rather than an offensive move. When we actually get to portfolio design and security selection in Chapters 8 and 9, you'll see how this notion of "timing the market" can be put into practice on a personal level.

Plotting Your Personality

All that having been said, let's get back to our Market Timing-Money Management (Spontaneity) line. I've shown this one vertically. Plot yourself on this line.

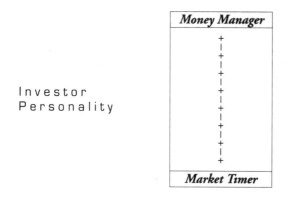

Now let's put the two lines together and see if we can develop anything useful.

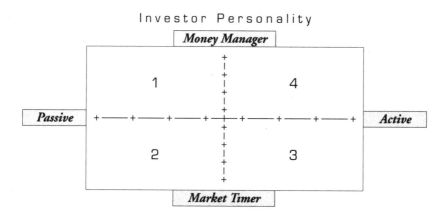

Obviously, by crossing the two lines, we have created four quadrants, which could generally be labeled 1) Passive Money Manager, 2) Passive Market Timer, 3) Active Market Timer and 4) Active Money Manager.

Refer back to the positions you initially plotted for yourself on the Involvement and Spontaneity lines when they were separate. Mark those same positions on the four-way diagram. Now, just like on the back of a cereal box, connect the dots! Draw a horizontal line from your spot on the Spontaneity axis to intersect with a vertical line drawn from your position on the Involvement axis, like so:

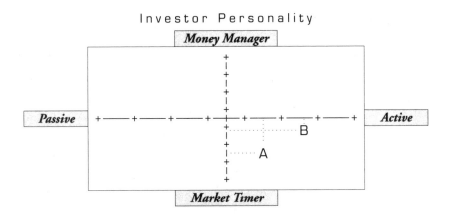

Investor Personality

Put a big star on the intersection. This will give you some idea of your investment personality. In the example above, the investor at position "A" would be described generally as an "Active Market Timer." This is not particularly scientific, I know, and again illustrates a tendency only. Most people could not accurately be placed at the extreme outer limits of any of the quadrants. So if you happened to end up, for example, as an "Active Market Timer" and you say, "That sort of describes me but I'm not really interested in being intimately involved on a day-to-day basis in my investment portfolio," don't worry. This is a general assessment only. Look at position B. That person would also be termed an "Active Market Timer" but, though investor B obviously wants to be more actively involved than investor A, investor B is less enamored by market timing. Furthermore, if you disagree strongly with the implications of being in the quadrant where you find your result, go back to the original lines and review how you have plotted yourself. Change whatever you wish as long as you are honest with yourself – again, it is *your* personality we're talking about.

In fact, I would expect to find most investors clustered somewhere around the middle of the diagram because very few of us, particularly as typical Canadian investors, represent any of the extremes. And remember, there is no right or wrong place to be. Successful investors can be found in all four quadrants. It may also help you if I describe the four personalities a little more fully.

The Passive Money Manager

If you were a television watcher in the 1960s, you surely recall the show *Father Knows Best*. That show's title might be an appropriate description of the way the Passive Money Manager thinks successful investing is accomplished. People with this preference favour a well thought out, not-too-spectacular-yet-sound approach. They want advice from someone who has earned their respect by demonstrating an understanding of individual needs and who follows a well-defined methodology. They believe that risk management is important and that an asset allocation strategy will result in a more consistent rate of return even though that return may not be as "thrilling" as that of a 100 percent stock portfolio during major market advances. On the other side of the coin, returns will not be as devastating when markets decline. Once Passive Money Managers have established a trusting relationship with an advisor, they are quite willing to give that advisor a relatively free hand to carry out the mutually-agreed-upon plan. Popular investment choices for this type of investor are asset allocation or balanced mutual funds which invest in cash, bonds and equities at the discretion of a portfolio manager, who normally stays within prescribed ranges in each asset class.

The Passive Market Timer

A combination of simplicity and the promise of excitement appeal to the Passive Market Timer. They want in on the action but don't wish to make decisions themselves as to where that action is. They don't want to do their own research so they, too, have to find a "trusted" advisor. On the downside, this approach doesn't easily accomodate the development of a long-term strategy and, consequently, may not truly reflect personal risk tolerance because it focuses on return rather than risk.

Investors of this type are the favoured clients of active brokers and purveyors of tax shelters. Not wanting to be left out of anything that's "hot," these people are sometimes easy prey for the "get rich quick" artist. They are also the most likely to subscribe to market timing services or newsletters.

The Active Market Timer

The plus side of the "Active Market Timer" stance is that it allows investors to take advantage of the latest potential "big winner." Provided they are accurate in their timing, they can make some quick money by being in and out of the deal. The challenge, of course, is to know exactly when to get in and out.

Investors favouring this method will often use discount brokers to carry out their stock transactions because the frequency of activity would otherwise lead to unduly high transaction costs. Because they do their own research, however, they do not require the services of a full brokerage firm. They also enjoy "flipping" real estate, trading commodities and speculating on business deals.

The Active Money Manager

If understanding, control and long-term wealth accumulation are the key features you seek, then the "Active Money Manager" school of thought is the one to which you belong. You'll be able to construct a portfolio which addresses your risk tolerance and, once established, leaves you more or less free to do other things, just checking in once in a while to make sure things aren't too much off track.

The disadvantage of this method is that it requires more work. It is vital to spend time assessing your risk tolerance, setting long-term objectives and matching investment alternatives to your needs. This is not a responsibility you can abdicate to someone else if you truly want to make it work for you.

Oh, and one more thing – this approach isn't particularly exciting. In fact, it can be quite boring. Once the research is done and the plan put in place, there isn't much more to do, except check in periodically to ensure everything is still on track and amend as necessary.

Spelling Out Your Philosophy

By now, then, you should have a fairly good handle on your personal investment philosophy. Let's put all three components together and see what things look like for you. The three areas for evaluation were:

1) Risk tolerance,

2) Involvement (Active/Passive) and

3) Spontaneity (Market Timer/Money Manager).

Now I want you to rank yourself on the three scales by writing two or three words for each that describe your view of your investment philosophy:

Risk –
_____
(Very Low ————————————— Very High)

Involvement –
_____
(Passive ——————————————Active)

Spontaneity –
_____
(Market Timer ———————————Money Manager)

Some examples would be:

Risk –   *moderatley high*
_____
(Very Low ————————————— Very High)

Involvement –   *somewhat active*
_____
(Passive ——————————————Active)

Spontaneity –   *favour money management*
_____
(Market Timer ———————————Money Manager)

The Investment Statement – Four Parts

The activities of the past few pages are leading us towards the creation of what I call the "Investment Statement." What we have just completed is the first stage of its development: Level 1 – Personal Philosophy. In total, the Investment Statement has four parts to it:

Level 1 – Personal Philosophy
Level 2 – Investment Objective
Level 3 – Asset Allocation
Level 4 – Security Selection

While the mere fact that this is a four-part exercise may seem a little intimidating, please be patient. We'll go through it one step at a time and you'll quickly see that it is not that onerous and actually quite useful. You'll find that a "qualitative and quantitative statement" such as you are going to develop will give you a clear idea of how to structure your portfolio to ensure it addresses current needs and long-term objectives. In addition, it will become your "guiding light" by providing a frame of reference for future investment decisions. Whenever something new comes along – a new project, a new investment proposal – you'll be able to evaluate it within the context of the goals you've set. If the new opportunity complements what you are doing, then you can feel free to explore it further. If it detracts from what you're trying to accomplish, you can quickly reject it. The Investment Statement makes decision-making efficient and effective.

The Investment Pyramid

Before we move on to the next level, it is probably worthwhile to introduce here another concept which may make our progress easier. I am referring to the ubiquitous investment pyramid.

I use the word "ubiquitous" because four out of five investment books you read will have some sort of a pyramid in them. It is used to show the structure of a "balanced" portfolio, the "risk / reward trade-off," and to detail the steps to building wealth. I'm not too proud to admit that as tired as I am of seeing it, the pyramid is undoubtedly the best way to illustrate all those things – so I'll use it too.

The purpose of my application, ostensibly at least, will be to depict the four levels of the Investment Statement. In doing that, however, I will inevitably touch on the other possibilities. Here, then, is my pyramid:

Level 4	*Security Selection*
Level 3	*Asset Allocation*
Level 2	*Investment Objective*
Level 1	*Personal Philosophy*

We've just dealt with Level 1, your personal investment philosophy, and we will refer back to it a little later. It is the base, the anchor, the foundation and the strength for everything which rests on top or comes after it. Thus it is vitally important that you agree with the assessment of you by you so far. If there is still doubt in your mind that you have thought through the basic questions raised by this chapter sufficiently to have come up with a picture of you the investor, you may want to stop right here, go back and try again.

The Investment Statement is something you are going to refer to from time to time, to provide an ongoing point of reference for your decision making. Additionally, if you do work alongside a financial planner or investment advisor on this project, it can become a "contract," so to speak, between you. It will spell out the mutual expectations with respect to your investment philosophy, objective, targeted return and portfolio structure. Because this can be such a valuable tool, it is worthwhile ensuring that, in fact, it does reflect the way you really feel about the entire investment process. I encourage you, therefore, to review the few words you wrote out earlier about risk, involvement and spontaneity. If you are satisfied with them, take a few minutes to re-write them in a narrative form. This will complete Level 1 of the Investment Statement. Here are a few Sample Level 1 statements to give you an idea of what I am suggesting:

> "I am a *moderately risk-tolerant* investor who wants to be *somewhat involved* in a *money management* approach to accumulating assets."

> "I have *high risk tolerance* and want to be *very active* with my own *market timing* ideas for maximizing return."

> "I am very busy and, thus, willing to *rely on the recommendations of others. I will let them do what they think is best for me* provided they take into account my need for *safety and security.*"

Now try your own:
"My personal investment philosophy could be described as

_____

_____

_____

_____

_____
                                                      ,,
_____

Let's move on then to Level 2 - setting the Investment Objective.

Summary

- *A rational investor will take on greater risk if the anticipated reward is sufficient.*
- *Your risk profile can change as your personal situation does.*
- *A survey of large pension plans proved conclusively that over 90 percent of a portfolio's investment result was determined by the asset allocation. Less than three percent of the performance could be attributed to market timing and, in some cases, the impact of timing attempts was actually negative.*
- *Market timing attempts to maximize return without regard for the psychological battering which transferring in and out of the various asset classes inflicts on the investor.*
- *Like most investment strategies, market timing can be practiced in degrees and in fact, somewhere between tactical market timing and equally purist fundamental money management lies a "strategic" position which would likely serve investors well.*
- *Four investor "personalities:*
  Passive Money Manager
  Passive Market Timer
  Active Market Timer
  Active Money Manager

- *There is no right or wrong place to be on the Investment Personality Diagram because successful investors can be found in all four quadrants.*
- *Your investor philosophy is a function of your risk tolerance and personality.*
- *A written Investment Statement becomes a frame of reference for decision-making.*
- *The four parts of an Investment Statement are:*

  Level I   Personal Philosophy
  Level II   Investment Objectives
  Level III   Asset Allocation
  Level IV   Security Selection

Chapter Seven:
Setting Your Objectives

INVESTING INVOLVES COMPROMISE AND IS OFTEN LESS A MATTER
OF WHAT YOU WANT THAN WHAT YOU ARE WILLING TO GIVE UP.

The Three Major Objectives

There are a lot of different words or terms that could be used to describe investment objectives. In my opinion, however, when all is said and done, all objectives, in one way or another, come down to *growth, income* or *liquidity.* Despite all the ancillary reasons stated for accumulating and distributing wealth, such as retirement, funding of children's education, paying off the mortgage, preserving estate values for heirs and so on, everything still boils down to these three fundamental objectives. We want our assets to *grow in value* – to be worth more at some point in the future than they are today; we want our accumulated wealth to be converted into *income to replace our working wages;* or we want to have a *liquid source of funds* to get us through emergencies or to allow us to take advantage of opportunities.

Objectives Can Change

Having so neatly reduced all investment objectives to these simple three, however, it is fair to say that, for most of us, our overall plan design will incorporate some element of each. Few of us will have situations so straightforward that we can think in terms of one objective only. Furthermore, our objectives can change as time passes and new priorities and influences shape the way we view the future. Let's look at the table below:

Investment Objectives Vary with "Life Stage"

Age	Primary Objective	Secondary Objective
20s	Liquidity	Income
30s	Income	Growth
40s	Growth	Growth
50s	Growth	Growth
60s	Income	Growth
70s	Income	Liquidity

When I look at this table, I can, to a large extent, see the way my life unfolded with respect to my personal financial objectives. For example, when I was in my early 20s, the most pressing financial concern in my life was the amount of money I had in my pocket on Saturday night so I could go out and have a good time. That was obviously a *liquidity* objective. My *time horizon* was very short – about a week! Unfortunately, there was no easy source of money for me so I had to earn what I wanted to spend, thus *income* become a secondary objective. It wasn't really an investment objective in the truest sense of the word except I suppose I was investing my time and effort. And the more I invested the more I got to spend!

By the time I got into my 30s, the priorities were very different. While it was still important to have ready access to cash, being in good health and in a good career position, I was less concerned with liquidity. I knew that if I really needed some cash beyond my fledgling savings, I could probably get it by simply signing my name on a bank loan application form. A properly balanced insurance program would ease the financial burden of most major catastrophes.

I am not, by the way, advocating here a reliance on borrowed money for all your liquidity needs. Prudence dictates that you must have some cash available for small financial surprises. But too many financial planning books that I have read insist on very large cash balances before beginning an investment program. The problem with that approach, as wisely cautious as it might be, is that very few people have the discipline to actually keep those free dollars in the bank. We *spend* money on things we *need;* we *save* money for things we *want.* Human nature being what it is, however, we are too easily capable of reclassifying *wants* into *needs.* When we see something which we suddenly decide we need and the money is easily accessible, our best intentions can go out the window. As David Chilton, author of the mega best-seller book *The Wealthy Barber* says, "A *need* is a *want* your neighbour already has!" It is simply too tempting, in my experience, to keep extra large amounts of readily obtainable money around.

Managing Debt

Certainly any debt has to be manageable and that includes the intelligent use of credit cards. The key words are "manageable" and "intelligent." Judicious use of credit can provide financial leverage to accelerate the accumulation of wealth; however, one also has to recognize that using other people's money for investments, for example, increases the risk. In fact, it may increase the risk to the point where it is outside your comfort zone, so you absolutely must evaluate the reward trade-off even more carefully if you are considering using borrowed money. If the investment sours, you may have lost not only some of your own money, but also some of the bank's. Bankers tend to be less understanding and patient than perhaps you yourself might be. Here is another handy "rule of thumb" to help you decide if "leveraged" investments are for you. The rule is simply this: every dollar you borrow to invest alongside your own increases your risk by 100%. So, for example, if you have $10,000 to invest and you borrow an additional $10,000, you *double* the risk. Therefore, if the chosen investment would normally yield, say, 10 percent, you should expect a return somewhere in the area of 20 percent to account for the extra risk. The mandatory question to ask yourself before making such an investment is "Do I want to invest in something that could potentially earn me 20 percent knowing that it is twice as risky as a 10 percent investment?" In other words, is a 20 percent investment within your "comfort zone"?

The ratio holds true for leveraged investments of higher or lesser proportions. For example, if you match your own money with 50 cents of the bank's, your expected return should be at least 50 percent higher than if you went it alone, that is, 15 percent; $10,000 of your own and $20,000 from the bank – 200 percent additional risk – should get 30 percent return, and so on. And then, of course, the really big one: none of your own funds with 100 percent leverage. In my opinion, that is at least four times as risky, so, in this example, I'd want to look at a 40% minimum potential return and see how that fit with my tolerance for risk.

Okay, back to me and my glorious 30s! With liquidity retreating as the most important financial objective in my life, what moved forward to take its place was *income*. The reason was simple: the decade of my 30s was, for me, largely an acquisitory stage of my life. Marriage had brought with it a much greater interest than a bachelor would normally perceive as necessary in the comforts of home – things like furniture, a larger car, a well-stocked refrigerator, vacations and certainly not to be neglected, the house itself!

Unfortunately all of those material goods had to be paid for and bearing in mind the need for careful use of credit, that meant cash flow or income became the factor which governed how quickly assets of any type could be accumulated.

But something else was happening. Some of that income was being employed to acquire things that actually began to appreciate in value. Most notable, of course, was the family dwelling, but there were, whether by good luck or good planning, a few smaller items that gained in value. We are not talking megabucks here. But the first $1,000 Canada Savings Bond purchased on the payroll deduction plan, a good life insurance program, a minimum monthly automatic bank deposit to an RRSP account – all of these things slowly began to add to personal net worth. So *growth* emerged as a secondary objective during that stage of my life.

And now, since I am not too many years beyond age 40, I'll have to generalize about the next significant shift in primary investment objective. This change usually takes place during the 20 or so years between the approximate ages of 40 and 60. This period represents, for many of us, our "peak earning years" when we are well along in job or career, with incomes progressing towards their upper limits. Financial responsibilities often begin to decline as children become self reliant, mortgages are paid down or off, most material needs have been pretty much met and disposable income generally rises. Coupled with climbing values of earlier investments and savings plans, this is a time of relative financial easing and probably provides the greatest opportunity to accumulate wealth. *Growth*, therefore, becomes the watchword.

As we move towards age 60, once again there is likely to be a refocusing of purpose. We now want those assets which we have been accumulating for the previous 15 or 20 years to be converted to *income* to supplement pensions, government benefits and such. Recalling, though, our earlier admonition about allowing for the inflation which will not disappear after retirement, we must have our amassed assets continue to *grow*, at least at a rate equal to increases in the cost of living.

And then, finally, the latter years of age 70 and beyond will often prompt us to think about those who will survive us and how we might pass whatever assets we don't use ourselves onto them efficiently, so estate *liquidity* emerges, at least as a secondary objective.

So there you have it – your life (and mine) all neatly laid out. Of course, we know that everything I have just said is not precisely the way it happens to everyone. On an individual level, people seldom behave as the masses do, but from their *combined* behaviour we can identify tendencies, and that is what we are dealing with here. The "life stages" described above are broad generalizations. The ages and their corresponding primary and secondary objectives are not cast in stone. We all know people who are well along in their wealth-building programs before they reach age 30 and, regrettably, we know others who are not likely to ever accumulate even a small amount of surplus cash.

The essential message here, however, is that our objectives can change over time. Consequently, any investment strategies we develop should reflect our current goals and yet not be so rigid as to preclude altering them if our priorities shift. Suitability and flexibility – that's what we want.

Investment Objectives and the Basic Asset Classes

Having now established that, despite the popularity of a thousand other descriptive words, *growth, income* and *liquidity* are really the only investment objectives one might have, you may have already jumped ahead and made the logical connection between those three objectives and the basic asset classes. That link-up looks like this:

Objective	Asset Class
Growth	Equity
Income	Debt
Liquidity	Cash

Again this relationship is not a perfect one. As described before, in addition to debt instruments, some equity assets provide income in the form of dividends or rent and certain cash-type holdings yield interest regularly, but, in general, if we think of growth as being a primary objective, then equities offer the greatest growth prospects. Debt instruments are normally set up to provide regular income flows and cash-type assets are most liquid.

Re-introducing the sample investments that we have chosen to represent the various asset classes, they line up this way:

Objective	Asset Class	Investment
Growth	Equity	Stocks
Income	Debt	Bonds
Liquidity	Cash	T–Bills

It is important to restate at this juncture, however, that the T-Bills, bonds and stocks were chosen as approximate measures for entire investment classes only for convenience. In real life and as a matter of good practice, a well-designed investment strategy would account for *all* of an investor's assets in their respective asset classes. For example:

Objective	Asset Class	Typical Investment
Growth	Equity	Common stocks, growth mutual funds, real estate, business interests, collectibles, precious metals
Income	Debt	Bonds, mortgages, fixed income mutual funds, preferred shares, loans, pension plans, government benefits
Liquidity	Cash	T-Bills, money market funds, term deposits, GICs, Canada Savings Bonds, bank accounts

In fact the truth is that, to a certain extent at least, almost all assets could be used for all objectives. It's just that some are obviously better suited than others for a particular desired outcome.

Developing Your Personal Objectives

In my travels and talks with financial planners throughout North America, the most frequently encountered concern among them is that many of their clients have portfolios that are too small to achieve all their goals *given reasonable assumptions about investment performance.* This state of affairs exists for two very simple reasons:

(a) investors wait too long to begin building assets and

(b) as a consequence of (a), the rate of return required to meet the investors' goals is too high.

The first of these is easy to understand. The sooner you start to accumulate wealth, the longer the miracle of compounding can work in your favour and the sooner you'll meet your objective. Let's look at a couple of examples (and don't worry if the numbers seem inappropriate for your personal situation. They were chosen simply to make the arithmetic easier. You can add or subtract zeros to approximate your personal situation):

Example #1

Target: To accumulate $1,000,000 for retirement

Rate of Return: 12% per year

Monthly Investment: $500

Age able to retire if started at 25 years old: 52

Age able to retire if started at 35 years old: 62

As you would expect, if you start 10 years later, there will be a 10-year difference in the age by which you will have met your target. The huge advantage, however, becomes evident if you think about what would happen during that extra ten years you would be retired, between age 52 and 62, had you started your accumulation program at the earlier age. Obviously, you would have an additional decade to enjoy retirement and enjoy it you could – because you would have ten additional years of income generated by the $1,000,000 you had accumulated. If, for example, you were able to continue to earn 12 percent per year on your investments after retirement (and if you earned 12 percent up to retirement, there is a good chance you could continue to do so), you could have a $120,000 a year retirement income without any encroachment on the capital. Let's see – $120,000 a year for 10 years – that's $1,200,000 of income foregone by waiting until age 35 to begin an investment program. That's real money!

Example #2

Target: To accumulate $1,000,000 by age 60

Rate of Return: 12% per year

Monthly investment required from 25 years old: $200

Monthly investment required from 35 years old: $625

Again, a startling difference! You would have to contribute more than three times as much on a monthly basis if you delayed. What's more, the 25-year-old would have put away a total of about $87,000 over the 35 years to age 60; the 35-year-old would have had to set aside about $100,000 more (approximately $187,500 in total) to end up with the same amount of money at retirement.

Example #3

Target: To accumulate $1,000,000 by age 60

Monthly Investment: $500

Rate of return required if started at 25 years old: 8%

Rate of return required if started at 35 years old: 12%

While one could easily look at these percentages and conclude that 12 percent is as attainable as eight percent, the point is that 12 percent is one and a half times higher than eight percent. Wouldn't the risk be proportionately higher as well? For a low-risk investor, even 12 percent might be too ambitious, given what we know about investment returns. Recall that the only investment of the three we have chosen (stocks, bonds and T-Bills) with a long-term track record of about 12 percent was stocks. Should we structure the portfolio of all 35-year-old investors entirely with stocks ? I hope you don't believe that or I have not done a very good job so far in this book of discussing risk management.

The Risk/Reward Trade-off – A Roleplay

It doesn't matter which way we look at it, does it? You must set your objective based on realistic expectations about your ability to save and invest and reasonable assumptions about investment returns.

Perhaps I can illustrate this point more effectively by walking you through a fairly representative dialogue between a good financial planner or investment advisor and a typical client. It might go something like this:

Advisor: *Okay, Bill, we have completed the financial planning part of the process. Now we want to put together an investment strategy which will help you reach your goals.*

Client: Sounds good to me – this is the bit I've been waiting for.

Advisor: *However, before we actually get down to designing your portfolio, Bill, I'd like to do one final check on my understanding of exactly what your goals are.*

Client: You have done a pretty thorough job. I am confident you understand me quite well. The most important goal is for me to be financially secure so that I can retire early. That's the big one.

Advisor: *Right – and you want to retire in about 15 years... around age 60, with an inflation-adjusted income, excluding government benefits, not too much lower than what you are earning today.*

Client: That's it – around $50,000 a year. I'm 45 years old and in good health. There are quite a few things I want to do in my retirement and most of them cost money. I can't see me really enjoying myself if my income were to drop suddenly.

Advisor: *All right, Bill, let's review what we concluded about your tolerance for risk or fluctuation in your investments. You felt....*

Client: I'm not really a risk taker, remember? I understand now that perhaps I have been a little too cautious in the past and that I'll need to expand my "comfort zone" as you called it – but not too far.

Advisor: *Of course not. In fact, on this Investment Statement I had you write out, you described yourself as "moderately risk tolerant." Do you still feel that way?*

Client: Yes, I think that would be a fair assessment. I had just never thought about managing risk in the way we've talked about it.

Advisor: *And in our earlier review of various investments such as stocks, bonds and T-Bills, we found that "moderately risky" investments had historical returns of, say, between eight and 12 percent. So could we describe your comfort zone as somewhere between eight and 12 percent?*

Client: Yes, I think so. I don't believe I would worry too much about investments such as the ones we've talked about with returns in that range. Also, I do remember the "fluctuation factor" impact, so I know that eight to twelve percent represents a normal range only. From time to time, returns for investments in that category may be higher or lower, but in the long run, they should average, say, 10 percent.

Advisor: *Good! So those are the assumptions on which I am going to proceed. You want to retire in 15 years with sufficient assets to generate a $50,000 a year income, adjusted for inflation. So your primary objective right now is* growth *changing to* income *at about age 60. And if we start off with a mix of investments which have a past track record of yielding about 10 percent on average with modest fluctuation, you won't lie awake at night worrying about them.*

Client: You've got it.

Advisor: *Okay. Let me plug these numbers into my computer here and see what we get. You have no company pension plan and we are ignoring government benefits because you want them to be a "bonus" if, in fact, on an after-tax basis, they are worth anything at all to you. You already have investments totalling about $50,000 and you've indicated that you could set aside an additional $500 a month between now and age 60 to help build up your capital. The desired income is $50,000 a year and we'll allow five percent for inflation. Okay computer, do your stuff!*

(10 seconds later)

Advisor: *Oh, oh!*

Client: What is it?

Advisor: *Well, it looks like, if we use these assumptions, to meet your stated retirement objectives, we are going to have to earn you an average of 15 percent per year on your investments.*

Client: Fifteen percent – so, can you do it?

Advisor: *Certainly, we do know of investments which have earned 15 percent in the past, but that is no guarantee for the future and...*

Client: So maybe we should look at those?

Advisor: *But wait a minute, Bill – what rates of return did we decide were within your comfort zone? It was from eight to 12 percent as I recall.*

Client: Yeah, but returns in that range obviously won't meet my needs... so I have to shoot for better yields and that means taking on more risk...

Advisor: *Or rethink your goals. Perhaps they are too high.*

Client: Well maybe they are a little ambitious – but they are where I'd *like* to be 15 years from now. Just how risky are those 15 percent investments?

Advisor: *It's hard to say because there aren't as many of them around as there are of the 10 percent variety and we have less historical data on them. I think it is fair to say, however, that if we expect them to generate a rate of return 50 percent higher than the ones we originally considered, we have to be prepared to increased risk of about the same proportion. How would you feel about that?*

Client: I like the 15 percent part – but I don't think I'd be comfortable with that much more risk. But obviously I have to get more than 10 percent or I won't even come close to my objectives.

Advisor: *How high do you think you'd be willing to go?*

Client: I guess I could live with investments which averaged 12 percent – the upper limit of my comfort zone.

Advisor: *In fact, that would expand your comfort zone. Investments which have averaged 12 percent also have a higher fluctuation factor. Are you prepared for that as well?*

Client: I don't really have a choice, do I?

Advisor: *Of course you do. As I said earlier, you could scale down your goals to ones which are achievable with a 10 percent average return...*

Client: Fifteen percent will meet my goals, but the risk is too high for my peace of mind. I'm comfortable with 10 percent, but that won't get me where I want to go. It's a trade-off then, isn't it?

Advisor: *Yes, Bill, that is exactly what it is. What level of risk are you willing to assume to get the reward you want?*

Client: Okay... Okay. Let's shoot for 12 percent. It's in between. I'll give up some potential return for less volatility.

Advisor: *Are you sure? You've got to really believe in this. If even 12 percent is going to bother you....*

Client: No. No. I can handle it. Let's look for investments which have earned about 12 percent on average over the long haul. Can't we can mix and match a few things to reduce the fluctuation?

Advisor: *Yes, we can. In fact, I'm hopeful that one or both of two things will happen. You'll end up with more than 12 percent average annual return. Obviously, we can't make any promises or predictions in that regard but if we balance the portfolio properly, we can improve the chances of hitting that target. The other possibility is that you'll find the volatility associated with 12 percent investments isn't too bad at all. You'll come back to me at some point and say, "I think I can manage a little more risk now." Then we can re-evaluate the investment choices we originally made and perhaps look for something a bit more aggressive. How does that approach sound to you?*

Client: Sounds okay. What investments are you recommending?

Okay, it is time to step back into the real world. Although the preceding was obviously an overdramatization, it illustrated a couple of very important concepts:

1) Given reasonable market assumptions, most portfolios are too small to achieve all an investor's goals.

2) It may be possible to structure a portfolio with a target rate of return which will meet objectives, but the volatility (risk) may be too high.

3) It is usually better to focus on *risk* rather than *return*.

4) Once your risk tolerance is established, it sets an upper limit on the portfolio's long-term expected rate of return.

5) If the rate of return is inadequate to meet your objectives, then those objectives have to be scaled down or your willingness to commit more money to the task must be increased.

As a matter of interest, in the foregoing example, assuming a 12 percent average rate of return, Bill's retirement objective could largely be met if he were able and willing to do any one of the following:

1) Invest an additional $ 68,000 up front.

2) Invest $1,250 a month rather than $500.

3) Retire at age 67 rather than age 60.

4) Accept $29,000 a year income instead of $50,000.

Getting Professional Help

Perhaps none of those alternatives by themselves will be desirable. The best answer may be some combination of all of them, that is, a modification of the objectives overall. It becomes a matter of compromise and is often less a matter of what you *want* than what you are willing to *give up*. Except in those rare cases where your assets are greater than required to meet your goals, it is necessary to weigh the options and outcomes. The resulting portfolio should be the one which best balances objectives and tolerance for risk.

In this regard, because this is a negotiative process and because it is difficult to negotiate from both sides of the table, I strongly urge you to consult a professional financial planner or investment advisor to help you through the process. The services of a well-trained, objective outsider can go a long way towards improving the likelihood of meeting your aspirations. For example, in our little role play, we did not consider leverage programs or how to improve after-tax yields as additional methods of moving closer to the targeted returns, yet these are viable alternatives which are best considered under the watchful eye of a competent specialist.

If you are not already familiar with an advisor whom you respect and trust, ask your friends and colleagues or contact one of the professional financial planning trade groups such as the Canadian Association of Financial Planners for a referral. I also encourage you to read up on the subject yourself so that you can judge whether or not the financial planner can bring value to the relationship. Once you have identified a planner whom you think you might engage, ask that individual to demonstrate his or her competence, for example by showing you plans completed for others, by outlining the steps followed in developing such a plan and by showing how he or she arrived at specific investment recommendations. In return, you should be prepared to disclose the details of your financial circumstances as they are today and provide some insight into your thinking about the future. If you are both honest, at the end of an initial meeting, you'll know whether you can be a team.

Some caution is warranted here, however. Regrettably, in terms of who does what, the financial planning industry is not an easy one to sort out. There are some participants who are really product purveyors only. There is nothing wrong with that if all you are looking for is an investment product specialist. Perhaps you are towards the extreme "active" end of the Involvement line we reviewed earlier, an "Active Market Timer," and all you require is someone to carry out your self-directed plans. Marketers of the investment products you may need are compensated either through salary (banks, trust companies) or commission (mutual fund salespeople, stock brokers, insurance agents, etc.).

At the opposite end of the spectrum from the product specialists are the "fee only" financial planners, who perhaps make no product recommendations at all or who will, after completing your financial plan, refer you to a product specialist. As the description implies, these practitioners are paid for their time, on an hourly or flat-fee basis. The most frequently cited reason for using a "fee only" planner is that they profess to offer independent advice, unbiased towards any particular product because they are compensated by the client rather than the product supplier. This may or may not be true. It still comes down to the integrity and competence of the planner.

In fact, I have seen both good and not-so-good plans prepared by planners under every conceivable compensation arrangement. From a simple volume perspective, the majority of plans have been done by people who are paid on a commission basis or perhaps on a "fee plus commission basis," probably because there are many more individuals in the financial planning industry working on a commission basis than there are earning fees or salaries only. In my opinion, the commission method of payment has made professional financial planning available to many more investors than would be the case if everyone had to pay up-front fees. You can decide which is best for you. The important thing is that you know early in the process how the planner you want to deal with will be paid. Equally important, in my opinion, is that you have a relationship with someone you trust and in whom you have confidence. Personally, I would want a planner who stood behind *both* the plan and the product. With that in mind, it is appropriate to say a few words about the interdependence of the investment strategy and the financial plan itself, that is, the *product* and the *plan*.

Investment Strategy and the Financial Plan

Simply put, it is impossible to make intelligent asset-allocation decisions without *first* considering an overall financial plan. The investments are merely *tools*, vehicles for carrying out the financial plan. In developing that plan, you will set out philosophies, goals, objectives and constraints. In choosing appropriate investments, you must match them to the parameters developed in the financial plan. Let's take an example. Say the *financial* objective is to retire in 20 years. The corresponding *investment* objective, then, would be to accumulate assets for 20 years (Growth) so they can be systematically liquidated over the 20 to 30 years of expected retirement (Income). The financial plan would identify the *amount* of income desired at retirement, the available assets with which to work, the manageable ongoing deposits and the capital required to meet the objective. The investment strategy would determine the asset allocation most likely to obtain rates of return which were required to meet the target. The portfolio would then have to be adjusted to balance the required rates of return and the level of risk that the investor was willing to assume.

Individual investor background will also have a bearing on the asset allocation. It seems pretty clear, for example, that if you are an entrepreneur, the value of your business is obviously a very important asset. It provides income, tax shelter and increase in net worth over time. Obviously your asset allocation, in that case, will be different from, let's say, the much-maligned government worker who has a very secure and relatively high-paying job. If I was to ask that person what his or her financial goals were, the response would probably be something like, "to retire early" or "to educate my children" or "to pay off the mortgage." In either situation, the tools used to accomplish the objectives – the stocks, bonds, bank accounts or whatever – are just that: tools. By themselves, they are merely different places to put money, but properly aligned with sound, achievable financial objectives, they become powerful building blocks to successful wealth accumulation.

We have come a long way in this chapter and have now climbed through Level 2 of our investment pyramid.

| Level 2 | | *Investment Objective* |
| Level 1 | | *Personal Philosophy* |

To maximize the value of what we have just done, go back to the Level I part of the Investment Statement you wrote in Chapter 6. Rewrite it here and add a few words for Level 2 — state your investment objective, in terms of *growth, income* and/or *liquidity.*

Here are samples of Level 2 statements:

"My primary investment objective is *growth* over the next twenty years. I do not anticipate a need for income from my portfolio prior to that time, although I would like to have some funds available for emergency or opportunity."

"Within five years I wish to begin receiving an annual income from my investments to supplement my company pension. I also recognize the need for growth beyond retirement to off-set inflation."

"My portfolio should be largely made up of *liquid* assets so as to facilitate an efficient transfer to my heirs."

Now add your own Level 2 statement to what you wrote in Chapter 6:

Level 1

_____

_____

_____

Level 2

_____

_____

_____

Now that you have defined your personal investment philosophy and spelled out your objectives in terms of growth, income and liquidity, it is time to move up one more step on the pyramid, to Level III — Asset Allocation.

Summary

- *The three basic investment objectives are* growth, income *and* liquidity.
- *Our objectives can change as time passes and new priorities and influences shape the way we view the future.*
- *There is a logical connection between the three objectives and the basic asset classes:*

Objective	Asset Class
Growth	Equity
Income	Debt
Liquidity	Cash

- *Use of credit can provide financial leverage to accelerate the accumulation of wealth but using other people's money for investments increases the risk.*
- *Given reasonable market assumptions, most portfolios are too small to achieve all an investor's goals.*
- *It may be possible to structure a portfolio with a target rate of return which will meet objectives, but the volatility (risk) may be too high.*
- *It is usually better to focus on* risk *than* return.
- *Once your risk tolerance is established, it sets an upper limit on the portfolio's long-term expected rate of return.*
- *If the rate of return is inadequate to meet your objectives, then those objectives have to be scaled down or your willingness to commit more money to the task must be increased.*
- *Investing involves compromise and is often less a matter of what you* want *than what you are willing to* give up.
- *It is impossible to make intelligent asset-allocation decisions without* first *considering an overall financial plan.*

Chapter Eight:

Allocating Your Assets

IT IS USUALLY BETTER TO FOCUS ON RISK THAN RETURN.
BY SETTING AN UPPER LIMIT ON THE AMOUNT OF
RISK YOU ARE WILLING TO ASSUME, YOU AUTOMATICALLY PUT
A CEILING ON THE RATE OF RETURN YOU CAN
REALISTICALLY EXPECT TO EARN FROM YOUR PORTFOLIO.

Now comes the part for which most readers have been willing to endure the previous seven chapters: actually allocating assets within a portfolio. Before we get into it, though, there is a little more preliminary work to be done. We are developing a process that will serve you well, not only now, but for many years to come. As I have said before, it must be appropriate for you today and yet flexible enough to meet your changing needs. It is vital, therefore, that each step be thoroughly completed before the next one is begun. It's like building our pyramid; we can't start at the top and work down because each level has to be solid enough to support all those above it. I hope that by now it is becoming apparent that, as we move up the pyramid, we are making the transition from the *general* to the *specific*. Level III – Asset Allocation takes the concepts developed so far and puts them into action. The asset-allocation decisions you make in this chapter will be the framework for constructing your portfolio, but their long-term usefulness will be directly related to the strength of the underlying assumptions about your personal philosophy and objectives.

With these thoughts in mind, then, the asset allocation step is simply a matter of answering the following question:

> "Given my personal *philosophy* (risk tolerance and investor personality) and my *objectives*, what percentage of my assets should be allocated for *growth*, what percentage for *income* and what percentage for *liquidity?*"

Phrased this way, the question obviously focuses on the investment *objective*. If you prefer, it could also be re-stated in terms of the basic asset classes:

> "Given my personal *philosophy* (risk tolerance and investor personality) and my *objectives*, what percentage of my assets should be allocated to *equities*, what percentage to *debt* and what percentage to *cash?*"

Or, distilling it even further, using the three specific investments we have relied on so far, you could ask something like this:

> "Given my personal *philosophy* (risk tolerance and investor personality) and my *objectives*, what percentage of my assets should be invested in *stocks*, what percentage in *bonds* and what percentage in *T-Bills?*"

You are going to come to the same result, regardless of the approach you take. The important thing to note here is that we did not, in any of the above examples, waver from the underlying assumptions with respect to philosophy and objectives. The asset-allocation decision is founded on those two fundamentals, which are unique to you.

To keep things simple, I'm going to use the most specific version of this key question because it will allow me to quantify the outcome more readily. As before, feel free to substitute whatever you think are appropriate investments for you in place of the stocks, bonds and T-Bills I'll be using to illustrate the asset-allocation process.

The Traditional Portfolio

Let's begin by looking at what is typically referred to as a "traditional portfolio," that is, a portfolio split among the three major asset classes. The simplest method of doing that would be to use what I call "the naive approach": allocating one-third of the assets to cash (T-Bills), one-third to income (bonds) and one-third to growth (stocks). In fact, had you done that over the past 43 years of our data survey, you would have enjoyed an average annual return of about eight percent with a "fluctuation factor" of only seven percent. Not bad! Furthermore, you would have had negative returns only four years out of the 43 years between 1951 and 1993 with the worst being only -6 percent. That occurred back in 1974, which would also have been the last time you lost money in a single year. Such a track record would have gone a long way towards satisfying our newly developed aversion to loss.

So why wouldn't we suggest such a naive approach for everyone? I hope you already know the answer to that one. First, the eight percent average return may not appeal to more aggressive investors or to those whose objectives can only be met by achieving a rate of return in excess of eight percent. Secondly, it would have taken a tremendous amount of discipline to sit by and watch part of our portfolio earn extraordinarily high returns from time to time and not want to go chasing after them. For example, in 1961 our "naive portfolio" would have reached the outside limit of its "fluctuation factor" (8% ± 7%) when it yielded 15 percent overall — but the stock portion would have returned almost 35 percent! Human nature being what it is, it would have been awfully tempting then to beef up our stock holdings under the allure of those magnificent returns. However, had we done so, we would have seen the value of our equity holding fall by almost eight percent the very next year as the market declined. Similarly, in 1976, our naive portfolio would have gained over 13 percent but the bond portion would have contributed a return of almost 20 percent. 1990 would have netted us only five percent combined with the T-Bill component coming in at more than 13 percent average yield. With such variations it would have been a real mental challenge to stick with the one-third/one-third/one-third allocation through the ups and downs of the various asset categories.

That having been said, however, the "naive approach" may be just the ticket for some investors. In particular, I can see it appealing to those with a passive money management personality and low to moderate risk tolerance. You simply divide your assets equally into the three major asset classes and sit back waiting for them to grow. And they will... albeit somewhat more slowly than under certain other allocations, but with only modest fluctuations. If that type of performance meets your needs... go ahead! In fact, if this approach seems satisfactory to you and you wish to do so, you can skip through the rest of this book except for the bit in Chapter 10 about "Rebalancing." You should look at that because it tells you how to ensure that your portfolio does, in fact, remain in a balanced three-way split among cash, debt and equity holdings. On the other hand, if you are interested in how the overall portfolio return and volatility are determined and how more active investors might set up their portfolios, please read on because we are now going to pursue what I would call a more "traditional" approach to asset allocation, based on aligning objectives and realistic target rates of return.

Portfolio Weighting

So if you are still with us, let's proceed by supposing that you are a stereotypical 40-year-old with *moderate risk tolerance* whose personality favors the *money management* approach and your primary objective is *growth*. To me, that make-up would suggest the following:

a) Although your primary objective is growth, you wouldn't want all your money in stocks because the associated risk would be too high.

b) Yet, at age 40, your time horizon to retirement and beyond is sufficiently long to overcome the volatility associated with equity investments.

c) You wouldn't want too much of your money in T-Bills because that same extended time horizon opens cash-type investments up to the risk of eroding purchasing power due to inflation.

d) Because you believe in a money-management approach, diversification among assets is appealing. The emphasis, however, must be on equity-type investments because your primary objective is growth.

Given these conditions, then, your "traditional" portfolio might be structured something like this:

■ T–Bills	25%
▨ Bonds	25%
■ Stocks	50%
	100%

This mix puts one half of your portfolio in low-to moderate-risk investments and half in higher-risk assets. Is this the only or even the best asset allocation for this type of investor? Perhaps it is, but possibly not. What if, after thinking about this, you conclude that you want to seek out a higher return and yet you don't want to stray too far from your comfort zone? Then, because you know that stocks have the highest expected long term rate of return, you might alter the portfolio to increase the equity weighting, like so:

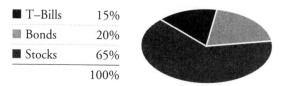

■ T–Bills	15%
▨ Bonds	20%
■ Stocks	65%
	100%

This allocation would put about two-thirds of your portfolio into the higher-risk category. Alternatively, what if you decide that your objective should be balanced a little more between growth and income? Simply re-adjust the percentages, perhaps as follows:

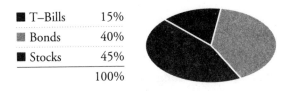

■ T–Bills	15%	
■ Bonds	40%	
■ Stocks	45%	
	100%	

As you can see, you can select the portfolio balance which best suits your risk tolerance, personality and objectives. If you want to "slant" the portfolio in one direction or another, simply increase and decrease the weightings of the appropriate investments. And keep two things in mind. First, the asset allocation you choose today is not the one you have to live with forever. It can be changed to reflect new attitudes or preferences as often as you like. Secondly, if your portfolio is sufficiently large and varied, you will likely want to consider the impact of shifting weightings among more than three investments. This is a "traditional" portfolio which reflects only three asset types but the theory can be readily extended to a "multiple asset" situation. Soon I'll be giving you some additional ideas on both aspects, that is, why and how to change asset weightings and dealing with a more broadly diversified portfolio. For now, however, let's continue with our simple example.

How Much in Each Class?

What we have done so far is fine as a conceptual exercise. But how do you, in the real world, decide *how much* to have in each asset category? What are the appropriate weightings? The answer to that can be as complicated or as simple as you choose to make it. For example, there are a number of sophisticated software packages that are designed to derive optimal portfolio balancing, given a number of input parameters. The problem I have with such programs is the old "garbage in – garbage out" deficiency of so many computer applications. The result will only be as good as the data on which the calculations are based. Since much of the input has to be some forecast of expected return and any such prognostication is, at best, an "educated guess," I'm not certain you will achieve much greater accuracy with computer-generated asset allocation than by following the approach developed so far. In addition, some programs that I have seen come up with a tremendous variance of result when only a small change of input is made. If the assumptions are off even slightly, the resultant weighting can be quite different from that which might be best for a particular investor.

At the other extreme, as we have seen, a straightforward split of a portfolio into one-third cash, one-third debt and one-third equities may result in not too bad an outcome – often better than many investors would achieve by themselves trying to follow market trends, their own intuition or the advice of others. But that kind of "blind" allocation may not fully reflect the risk tolerance or objectives of many investors. Predictably, then, the best response probably lies at a position somewhere between the two approaches. And perhaps an easy way to demonstrate this is think about what transpired in the earlier roleplay between the financial planner and Bill, the client. Clearly, in that scenario, there was a balancing act being performed between risk and reward, trading one off for the other until the optimum mix was achieved. Let's see the process in action.

Calculating Expected Return

Assume you have settled on the following asset allocation:

Treasury Bills	25%
Bonds	25%
Stocks	50%
	100%

The next step is to determine the expected rate of return for the portfolio by computing the weighted average of the returns for each investment. This sounds more complicated than it is. We developed the expected return for each individual asset in Chapter 3. All we have to do now is add together the proportionate return generated by each investment in the portfolio. The contribution of each asset is simply its expected return multiplied by the percentage of the portfolio it represents. The calculations would look like this:

Investment	(A) Expected Return	(B) % of Portfolio	(A) x (B) Weighted Return
T - Bills	7%	.25	1.8%
Bonds	8%	.25	2.0%
Stocks	12%	.50	6.0%
Total Portfolio Weighted Return			9.8%

So the weighted return of the portfolio is 9.8 percent. Let's call it 10 percent. That is the long-term average annual return we should expect with this asset allocation. That wasn't too bad, was it? Let's do the second half of the calculations.

Calculating Expected Risk

As we also identified back in Chapter 3, the second important dimension to investment performance is volatility. So now we want to examine the volatility of the *portfolio* as compared to the volatility of the individual assets. We do that by repeating the process above, this time substituting expected volatility for expected return. Again, we'll bring forward the numbers developed in Chapter 3.

| | (A) | (B) | (A) x (B) |
Investment	Expected Volatility	% of Portfolio	Weighted Volatility
T - Bills	± 4%	.25	± 1.0%
Bonds	± 10%	.25	± 2.5%
Stocks	± 18%	.50	± 9.0%
Total Portfolio Weighted Volatility			± 12.5%

In summary, if we combine these two results, we could say that a portfolio comprised of 25 percent T-Bills, 25 percent bonds and 50 percent stocks should have a long-term average annual return of approximately 10 percent with a fluctuation factor of about 12 percent. We would, therefore, expect the returns to range between -2 percent (10% - 12%) and +22 percent (10% + 12%). This would occur, on average, two out of three years, but occasionally they would be higher or lower (remember our definition of standard deviation: a two out of three probability that returns would fall within a certain range).

We still have not fully answered the question of *how much* of each asset we should have in our portfolio. Think back again to the vignette between Bill and his financial planner. The key message from that episode was that there had to be a trade-off between the risk Bill was willing to take on in his investments and the target rate of return he needed to meet his objectives. That is also our next step.

Juggling Risk and Reward

The more mathematically inclined reader will already be saying, "Hey, wait a minute, there is more than one way to come up with an average nine percent portfolio return or a 12 percent fluctuation factor!" And of course there is. For example, the following asset allocations all yield approximately the same overall portfolio return of about nine percent:

Portfolio One

Primary Objective – Liquidity
Secondary Objective – Growth

	(A)	(B)	(A) x (B)
	Expected Return	% of Portfolio	Weighted Return
■ T–Bills	7%	.50	3.5%
▨ Bonds	8%	.05	0.4%
■ Stocks	12%	.45	5.4%
Total Portfolio Weighted Return			9.3%

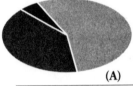

Portfolio Two

Primary Objective – Income
Secondary Objective – Growth

	(A)	(B)	(A) x (B)
	Expected Return	% of Portfolio	Weighted Return
■ T–Bills	7%	.05	0.4%
▨ Bonds	8%	.55	4.4%
■ Stocks	12%	.40	4.8%
Total Portfolio Weighted Return			9.6%

Portfolio Three

Primary Objective – Growth
Secondary Objective – Income

	(A)	(B)	(A) x (B)
	Expected Return	% of Portfolio	Weighted Return
■ T–Bills	7%	.15	1.0%
▨ Bonds	8%	.35	2.8%
■ Stocks	12%	.50	60%
Total Portfolio Weighted Return			9.8%

And what about the other concern — volatility? If we calculate the "fluctuation factor" for those same three portfolios, we come up with these numbers:

Portfolio #	Primary Objective	Secondary Objective	Volatility
1	Liquidity	Growth	+10.6%
2	Income	Growth	+12.9%
3	Growth	Income	+13.1%

Looking at these results, it is apparent that Portfolio #3 will likely fluctuate about 25 percent more than Portfolio #1 (13.1% vs 10.6%). If they both have the same expectation for return — about nine percent — you would probably opt for Portfolio #1, if risk was your major concern or your primary objective was liquidity. The general rule, therefore, is:

All other things being equal, if the expected returns are approximately the same, choose the portfolio with the lowest expected risk.

Of course intuitively, that makes sense, doesn't it? Why take on extra risk with no prospect of enhanced reward? Next question: Is the theory also valid the other way around, that is, looking at it from the volatility perspective? In general, yes it is, although on a more academic level, a simple weighted average calculation will overstate the actual risk of the portfolio. That's because of something called the "correlation coefficient" which we'll briefly touch on in the next chapter. For our purposes now, let's just assume the simplest case. Here are three . . .

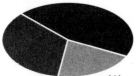

Portfolio One

Primary Objective – **Liquidity**
Secondary Objective – **Growth**

	(A)	(B)	(A) x (B)
	Expected Volatility	% of Portfolio	Weighted Volatility
■ T–Bills	4%	.40	1.6%
▨ Bonds	10%	.30	3.0%
■ Stocks	18%	.30	5.4%
Total Portfolio Weighted Volatility			± 10.0%

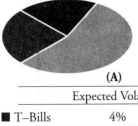

Portfolio Two

Primary Objective – **Income**
Secondary Objective – **Growth**

	(A)	(B)	(A) x (B)
	Expected Volatility	% of Portfolio	Weighted Volatility
■ T–Bills	4%	.20	0.8%
▨ Bonds	10%	.55	5.5%
■ Stocks	18%	.25	4.5%
Total Portfolio Weighted Volatility			± 10.8%

Portfolio Three

Primary Objective – **Growth**
Secondary Objective – **Income**

	(A)	(B)	(A) x (B)
	Expected Volatility	% of Portfolio	Weighted Volatility
■ T–Bills	4%	.35	1.4%
▨ Bonds	10%	.25	2.5%
■ Stocks	18%	.40	7.2%
Total Portfolio Weighted Volatility			± 11.1%

And if we tabulate the expected returns for these three portfolios, here is what we get:

Portfolio #	Primary Objective	Secondary Objective	Return
1	Liquidity	Growth	8.6%
2	Income	Growth	8.8%
3	Growth	Income	9.3%

Not a huge difference in absolute numbers, but an increase of almost one full percentage point of return, such as the difference between Portfolio #1 and Portfolio #3, will have a startling impact on asset accumulation over any reasonable time horizon. The conclusion, not unanticipated nor unlike what we decided earlier:

All other things being equal, if the expected risk is about the same, choose the portfolio with the highest expected return.

So, do we have a conflict here? I'm suggesting you choose on the one hand, the portfolio with the least risk and on the other, the portfolio with the greatest expected return. Of course we have a conflict. That's what this whole exercise is all about. To whatever degree of accuracy you desire, you can come up with a portfolio which approximates the level of risk you are willing to assume or the target rate of return necessary to meet your objectives. It is most likely, however, that these two portfolios will be mutually exclusive because, as we know, low risk and high return are seldom found in the same asset allocation. You'll have to do some trial and error number crunching to ultimately end up with the mix which is best for you.

So if we have two choices – to target return or to match risk tolerance – which one should you choose? Both will work; however, as you might suspect, my preference is to approach the asset allocation decision from the risk-management side rather than trying to put together a portfolio with an expected rate of return sufficient to meet my objectives. Here is my reasoning, which relates right back to our quest for "peace of mind" in investing.

Target Risk Rather Than Return

Let's suppose, for example, that you have a net worth of $10,000. You are sitting at home one evening reading the newspaper when you discover that your ticket in the provincial lottery just won $10,000. Your psychological well-being is going to be increased by your discovery. Right? Of course, you just doubled your net worth from $10,000 to $20,000! But what if your net worth was, say, $1,000,000, when you won the 10 grand? Your net worth, in that instance, would have increased by one percent to $1,010,000, so your *psychological* well-being would still go up — but not by as much as if you had a $10,000 net worth. More money is always better but the psychological lift we get from each additional dollar gets less and less. In other words, the dollar we already have is worth more to us than the dollar we have yet to receive.

Economists refer to this as the "declining marginal utility of wealth" — more money is always better but it is better at a diminishing rate. In an investment context, if we have the prospect of either gaining a dollar or losing one, we'd likely prefer to avoid the loss. For the sake of our "peace of mind," then, I prefer to do my asset allocation by focusing on risk rather than return. *By setting an upper limit on the amount of risk you are willing to assume, you automatically put a ceiling on the rate of return you can realistically expect to earn from your portfolio.* It is than a fairly straightforward matter of calculating the capital requirements necessary to meet your objectives using that rate of return. If the requirements are too onerous, objectives have to be scaled down, risk tolerance expanded or some combination of both.

With this background knowledge, it is now time for you to take a shot at writing out your Level III statement, identifying the basic asset allocation you feel will be within your risk tolerance and yet still address your objectives. I say "take a shot" because it is quite possible that the proportions for the three basic asset classes you set out now may well be changed at a point just a few pages further along in this book. Don't be alarmed by this. There is some "trial and error" to this process as we narrow our attention down to the specific assets you will have in your portfolio. That is why each time I ask you to write out a part of your investment statement, I also suggest that you go back and review what you have done for previous levels. As you gain more insight into the asset-allocation concept, you will probably be fine-tuning your thinking. So for now, draft the fundamental asset allocation which, based on what we have done so far, seems appropriate for your portfolio. Complete your Level III Statement by answering our question:

> " Given my personal *philosophy* (risk tolerance and investor personality) and my *objectives*, what percentage of my assets should be allocated for *growth* (or *equities*), what percentage for *income* (or *debt*) and what percentage for *liquidity* (or *cash*)?"

You will note that I have asked you to make this statement in terms of your objective or the three major asset classes only. We will identify the specific assets in Level IV. Following is a table of "suggested" portfolio balances, ranked by age, as compiled by one of Canada's leading accounting firms, to help you out a little further in deciding what might be the appropriate asset allocation for you. In a similar fashion to the "Objectives Vary with Life Stage" chart presented back in Chapter 4, these percentages are guidelines only, reflecting an academic view of the population at large. You must assign your own values in light of your personal Level I and Level II statements. Again you may find it a useful reminder to re-state those comments below. I have also offered some sample Level III statements.

Suggested Asset mix by Percentage (%)

Age	Cash	Debt	Equity
20s	35 - 50%	20 - 30%	20 - 35%
30s	10 - 15%	15 - 25%	60 - 80%
40s	5 - 10%	25 - 35%	70 - 80%
50s	5 - 10%	30 - 40%	50 - 60%
60s	20 - 30%	35 - 50%	20 - 35%

Sample Level III Statements

"My portfolio will be comprised of 20 percent liquid, 30 percent income and 50 percent growth assets."

"My portfolio will consist of 15 percent cash, 40 percent debt and 45 percent equity investments."

Now write out yours.

Level 1

_____

_____

Level 2

_____

_____

Level 3

_____

_____

_____

Let's climb to the top of the pyramid now and select some securities.

Summary

- *The asset allocation step is simply a matter of answering the following question:*

  "Given my personal *philosophy* (risk tolerance and investor personality) and my *objectives*, what percentage of my assets should be allocated for *growth*, what percentage for *income* and what percentage for *liquidity*?"

- *You can select the portfolio balance that best suits your risk tolerance, personality and objectives. If you want to "slant" the portfolio in one direction or another, simply increase and decrease the weightings of the appropriate investments.*
- *You can determine the expected rate of return for a portfolio by computing the weighted average of the returns for each investment.*
- *You can determine the expected risk of a portfolio by computing the weighted average of the volatility of each investment.*
- *All other things being equal, if the expected returns are approximately the same, choose the portfolio with the lowest expected risk.*
- *All other things being equal, if the expected risk is about the same, choose the portfolio with the highest expected return.*
- *It is usually better to focus on risk than return. By setting an upper limit on the amount of risk you are willing to assume, you automatically put a ceiling on the rate of return you can realistically expect to earn from your portfolio.*

Chapter Nine:

Selecting Your Securities

THERE IS FAR MORE TO THE POWER OF DIVERSIFICATION THAN
SIMPLY SPREADING YOUR ASSETS OVER A NUMBER OF INVESTMENTS
TO REDUCE RISK.

In this chapter, we will be adding the top layer to our pyramid. This is where you select the securities which will accomodate the asset allocation decisions made in Level III. As with just about everything we have discussed so far, you can incorporate as much detail into this part of the process as you wish. To a certain extent, however, the degree of sophistication will be influenced by the size of your portfolio. You can certainly apply the concepts to any amount of holdings, but as one might expect, the larger the asset base, the more opportunity there is to fully utilize these theories.

Broader Diversification Increases Return

Most investors understand that diversification reduces risk. The old adage "Don't put all your eggs in one basket" has been drilled into us for years. However, there is far more to the power of diversification than simply spreading your assets over a number of investments to reduce risk; you also want to have investments with different characteristics, that is different patterns of return which, ideally, occur at different times and under varying economic scenarios. Let me illustrate with a simple mathematical example.

Suppose you have $100,000 in cash and I offer you two options for investing the money. One is a choice of putting the entire $100,000 into a secure investment, perhaps a long-term government bond with a yield of, say, eight percent. The second option is to split the $100,000 into equal amounts of $20,000 and *diversify* among five investment opportunities with varying degrees of risk from, say, extremely risky to very conservative and with potential returns ranging, let's say, from zero to 15 percent. Specifically, the alternative investments are:

Amount	Investment	Expected Return
$20,000	Las Vegas	?%
$20,000	Under the Mattress	0%
$20,000	Term Deposit	5%
$20,000	Corporate Debenture	10%
$20,000	Mutual Fund	15%

If you choose the diversification route, you get to take $20,000 to Las Vegas and have a wonderful time. You might win but, if your experience is like mine, chances are the casino will come out ahead rather than you. You might think it odd for me to include a suggestion to gamble in Las Vegas in a book about investing for "peace of mind" but the profit potential there is really no worse than for a number of investments I have been exposed to and better than some. At least you can have some fun in Vegas as you lose your money! But if you accept my offer of diversification, this is part of the deal: you have to throw away the first 20 percent of your money! But then, realizing that you just blew twenty grand (albeit in search of a potentially big pay-off), you conclude that you had better be sure of *some* of your money, so you stuff the next $20,000 under your mattress to be left there until the day you need it. Obviously, money in such a "safe" place will not generate any return, but at least it will be there when you want it.

The third $20,000 you put into a Term Deposit at the bank,

assuming it will yield about five percent over time. Then, on the recommendation of your broker, you buy a good quality corporate debenture with an interest coupon paying 10 percent, using up another $20,000 and finally you allot the remaining $20,000 to a growth mutual fund which invests internationally and has a long-term track record of about 15 percent.

Given these two opportunities, which would you choose - the $100,000 bond investment earning eight percent or the diversified approach, knowing that you are going to lose the first $20,000, make nothing on the next $20,000 and only five percent on the third, ten percent on the fourth and fifteen percent on the last $20,000?

At first glance you might think, "Well, I enjoy Las Vegas but 'better a steady dime than a rare dollar'," so you select the non-diversified investment and, indeed, that might well be the best alternative for your particular risk profile. However, let me add one more element to our equation and that is that our time horizon is 25 years. Would that make a difference? Hopefully, you are nodding your head because you now agree that the long the *time horizon* the better choice certain investments, such as stocks (represented by the mutual fund in this example) become. So let's look at the actual results of choosing either of these options.

Amount	Investment	Return	Value in 25 Years
$100,000	Bond	8%	$684,500
$ 20,000	Las Vegas	-100%	$ 0
20,000	Mattress	0%	20,000
20,000	Term Deposit	5%	67,725
20,000	Debenture	10%	218,600
20,000	Mutual Fund	15%	658,375
$100,000			$964,700

By following the diversified approach, you would end up with about 40 percent more money despite the fact that the first two choices you made were, at best, duds! I admit, again, to choosing numbers that make the arithmetic work out more easily for me. However, the message is clear: diversification among properly chosen assets can increase return!

Broader Diversification Reduces Risk

The second part of the statement I made earlier with respect to the power of diversification was that it reduces risk. Let's see if I can demonstrate that.

Suppose that you have two investments which are identical in pattern of return, that is, they fluctuate to the same degree and as one goes up or down so does the other. The only difference is that one has a higher rate of return than the other. (Mathematicians refer to such a relationship as a "perfect *positive* cross correlation.") As a result of our previous discussions, you are, I hope, asking why we would bother to have two investments with equal risk when one has a greater reward than the other. Why not just keep the better-paying one? And indeed, that is the correct line of thinking because what we will end up with if we keep both investments is the *weighted average* of their returns and risk, right? We went through that exercise before so I won't bother with sample calculations here. This simple diagram, however, shows graphically what

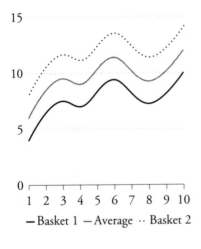

The Diversification Effect

Two Assets with Similar Patterns

— Basket 1 — Average ·· Basket 2

we are talking about. All we have done in this example is put our eggs in two similar baskets rather than one.

On the other hand, suppose we could find two investments with the same potential return but whose returns came at exactly *opposite* times, that is, as one went down, the other went up. (As you might expect, this relationship is technically called a "perfect *negative* cross correlation.") This diagram illustrates that situation. Again, the return would be the weighted average of the returns of the two investments but the risk now *would be completely eliminated!* All the negative returns of one would be offset by the positive returns of the other. What a marvellous situation!

The Diversification Effect

Two Different Baskets

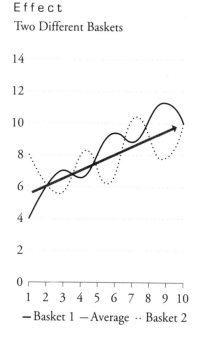

— Basket 1 — Average ·· Basket 2

Regrettably, in the real world, such a combination of investments doesn't seem to exist. If it did, all knowledgeable investors would never choose so-called "risk-free" assets, such as Treasury Bills. Instead they would look for two very risky investments with potentially high returns which occurred under exactly opposite market conditions. Putting them together would result in maximum return with no risk. The more likely situation is that larger portfolios will have a number of assets in them with *differing,* but not necessarily opposite, patterns of return. Then the results could resemble this:

Once more, the overall yield of the portfolio is the weighted average of the individual assets but the fluctuation – the risk – is dampened. It is, therefore, *possible to achieve a higher rate of return without increasing risk by building a multiple-asset portfolio.* This is the fundamental yet exceptionally powerful argument in favour of diversification.

With this as a background, let's continue along in the process of constructing a portfolio that is suited to you.

The Multiple Asset Portfolio

The Diversification Effect

Multiple Baskets

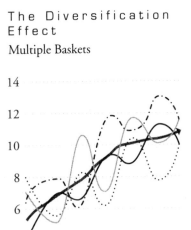

— Average

If your portfolio is relatively small, you may be satisfied with a simple diversification, as in our earlier examples, into something as straight forward as stocks, bonds and Treasury Bills. On the other hand, a larger portfolio offers more opportunity to enjoy the benefits of broader diversification just described. Integrating additional assets into a portfolio is not difficult and yet, properly done, can have a greater impact on overall portfolio return than any other decision, with the exception of the basic asset allocation into the three major classes.

We begin by assigning everything we would normally count among our investments to the three basic asset classes. Then we re-classify those categories to be more descriptive of the specific assets within them. Let me illustrate by taking on the role of a hypothetical investor whose net worth, grouped by asset class, is as follows:

Cash		Debt		Equities	
Bank Account	10%	Pension Plan	30%	Company Shares	30%
C.S.B.	5%	G.I.C.	10%	Mutual Fund	15%
	15%		40%		45%

I could quickly look at these figures and conclude that I have a relatively conservative portfolio with slightly more than one half of my assets in the low- to moderate-risk categories and the balance in higher-risk investments. However, to make this information more relevant and meaningful to me, I have to look *within* each asset class at the individual holdings. For example, my *cash* is split between my bank account and a Canada Savings Bond (remembering that I have previously classified CSBs as "cash" rather than "bond" type investments). Is there a significant difference between these two cash assets? Obviously, the answer is yes. As I am writing this, bank chequing/saving accounts are paying about three percent interest – while the just-announced new issue of Canada Savings Bonds offers seven-and-a-half percent for the first year – a significant advantage over the bank account. So should all cash holdings be in CSBs? No, because Canada Savings Bonds, money market mutual funds or whatever else I might decide to use for my cash investments have different characteristics than bank accounts. While all could be classified as "liquid," some are more readily accessible and therefore more appropriate as day-to-day drawing accounts. Others will serve as emergency or opportunity funds. The less liquid the cash asset is, the greater the interest rate I should earn.

Let's look at my *debt* assets. My pension plan represents the bulk of my investment in this category yet it is substantially different from my Guaranteed Investment Certificate. The pension plan is unavailable to me unless I retire or quit the firm (and then only with restrictions) and is itself probably quite conservatively invested, so let's suppose it is presently growing at a compound rate of about seven percent. GICs currently yield about nine percent and are more or less negotiable at any time.

Within the *equity* class, we will pretend my company shares came as part of a stock option plan I was given when I was contracted by the firm. However, the company has had mixed results over the past few years and the stock is now worth only about 20 percent more than its price when I bought it four years ago. I was able, though, to purchase the shares at a discount and the overall gain for me is about 40 percent. The only occasions upon which I am permitted to sell my company stock, however, are retirement or termination from the company. The mutual fund I own is invested in Canadian resource stocks and has lost about 15 percent over the past 24 months. My expectations for it were very high because it had a history of high volatility, moving up at a much faster rate than the stock market in general and I felt the time was right for strong performance from the resource sector. How do these investments – both equities – differ? The corporate shares are illiquid and exhibit low volatility while the resource mutual fund is quite liquid and has a large fluctuation factor.

With this information in hand, how do I proceed? Well, having first segmented the assets into the three basic categories, my next step is to subdivide the groupings into subsidiary components which more fully describe their nature and characteristics. That process might result in something which looks like this:

Cash		Debt		Equities	
Very Liquid		*Short Term*		*Conservative*	
Bank Acct	(10%)	GIC	(10%)	Stock	(30%)
Liquid		*Long Term*		*Aggressive*	
CSB	(5%)	Pension	(30%)	Fund	(15%)
Totals	(15%)	Pension	(40%)	Fund	(45%)

Schematically, this portfolio structure could also be shown in a "tree diagram" which would look like this:

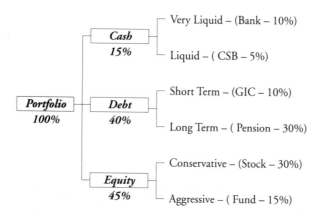

So we now have a better picture of what my hypothetical portfolio looks like. The next question is, "How will it perform?" To get the answer to that we simply follow the routine set out earlier, calculating expected return and volatility. As we go through the exercise with this portfolio, please bear in mind that the numbers used for the expected return and fluctuation factors of the assets in the portfolio are *my* "educated guesses." You and your advisor or financial product supplier will have to insert the appropriate figures for your personal investments. Using this sample portfolio, however, and my estimates, here is a tabulation of the expected results:

Expected Return

Asset Class	Investment	Expected Return	% of Portfolio	Weighted Return	Class Expected Return
Cash	Bank Acct.	6%	.10	0.6%	
	CSB	8%	.05	0.4%	1.0%
Debt	GIC	9%	.10	0.9%	
	Pension	7%	.30	2.1%	3.0%
Equity	Stock	10%	.30	3.0%	
	Fund	20%	.15	3.0%	6.0%
Total Expected Return					10.0%

Expected Volatility

Asset Class	Investment	Expected Volatility	% of Portfolio	Weighted Volatility	Class Expected Volatility
Cash	Bank Acct.	±3%	.10	0.3%	
	CSB	±4%	.05	0.2%	0.5%
Debt	GIC	±8%	.10	0.8%	
	Pension	±4%	.30	1.2%	2.0%
Equity	Stock	±15%	.30	4.5%	
	Fund	±20%	.15	3.0%	7.5%
Total Expected Volatility					10.0%

So with this portfolio mix, I should expect a long-term annual compound rate of return of about 10 percent with a fluctuation factor also of about 10 percent, that is, from zero percent (10% - 10%) to 20 percent (10% + 10%).

You can extend the concept through any number of assets, but obviously, the greater the range you have, the more calculations you'll have to make to derive the expected return and fluctuation factor. Recall, though, as I have stated several times already, that the result will only be as useful as you make it. It is essential to get the best information available with respect to the estimates of expected return and volatility for the particular assets in your own portfolio. Your personal experience, the background provided by your financial product salesperson and the counsel of other professional advisors should all be considered in arriving at meaningful figures. Remember, too, it is better to err on the negative side, underestimating return and overestimating risk. That way you are more likely to be surprised than disappointed.

Defining the Categories

Next question: "How do I decide which sub-categories to use?" The answer: "Use whatever is useful and meaningful to you." Pick ones that accurately describe the assets you are most likely to hold in your portfolio. In my own situation, I use the following:

Cash	– Very Liquid
	– Liquid
Debt	– Short Term
	– Mid Term
	– Long Term
Equity	– Conservative
	– Aggressive
	– Speculative

This arrangement covers all the assets I own in general enough terms to allow me to quickly classify them. It is also precise enough to permit me to "fine tune" my portfolio to a level of accuracy which is adequate for me. Remember: "approximately right rather than precisely wrong!" To show you how this can work, here is a broadly diversified and fairly aggressive sample portfolio. I haven't attempted to calculate expected return and volatility for this one because I'm sure you've got the idea by now. Please feel free to play with it yourself, however, if you would like the practice.

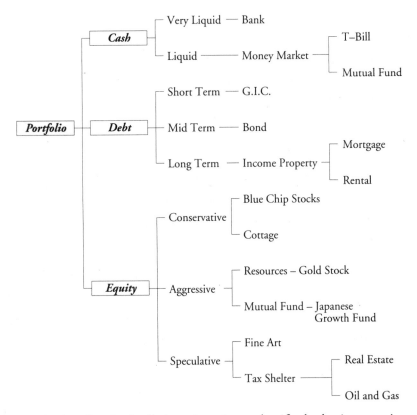

And really, that's all there is to it: re-classify the basic assets into meaningful sub categories, calculate expected return and volatility and write out your Level IV statement on "security selection." Here is a sample derived from the hypothetical portfolio presented earlier:

"My portfolio will have the following assets:

Cash	– Very Liquid	(10%)
	– Liquid	(10%)
		20%
Debt	– Short Term	(10%)
	– Long Term	(15%)
		25%
Equity	– Conservative	(20%)
	– Aggressive	(35%)
		55%

I expect an average annual return of approximately 10 percent with a fluctuation of about 10 percent, although it may
occasionally be higher or lower."

Or, if you wished, you could be even more specific by writing out
something like this:

"My portfolio will consist of my bank account (10%)
and a Canada Savings Bond (5%) for the liquid portion; my
pension plan (30%) and some GICs (10%) for the income
portion; and shares in my company (30%) and a resource
mutual fund (15%) for the growth portion.

With this mix, I expect my average annual return to be
about 10 percent with a range, two out three years, between
zero and 20 percent."

One more point here: the more specific you are, the more frequently you are going to have to review the Investment Statement. As we will
develop more adequately in the next chapter, the Level IV part is the
easiest to accomplish and subject to the most frequent change. As time
passes you will develop new preferences or alternatives for certain investments and want to incorporate or substitute them into your portfolio. If
you spell out exactly what your starting holdings are, you will have to re-

write the Level IV part of the Investment Statement each time you change securities. But that is not all bad and, in fact, it may be worthwhile to impose such discipline on yourself, because it should also result in your reviewing your Level I, II and III comments. I recommend investors re-examine their entire Investment Statement at least annually, so be as specific as you wish because there will be lots of opportunity throughout your investment time horizon to reshape your thoughts.

It is time for you to complete your Investment Statement in full by adding Level IV. Recall that I suggested in the last chapter that you might want to "fine tune" your Level III notes once you had a little more information, particularly as it applies to a multiple-asset portfolio. Here is your chance to do that.

Level I

_____

_____

_____

Level II

_____

_____

_____

Level III

_____

_____

_____

Level IV

_____

_____

_____

Keeping Tabs on Yourself

You should now have a complete Investment Statement. I encourage you to date and sign it, for a number of reasons. First, it will remind you of the time and context within which you made the decisions contained in it. If your thinking changes or any of the assumptions on which you based your choices subsequently becomes invalid (for example, the expected return or expected volatility of any of the assets turns out to be very different than anticipated), you will have a reference point from which to consider any amendments. In addition, as any new investment opportunity presents itself, you will be able to evaluate it in light of what you have written. If it appeals to you as an investment but doesn't seem to fit into the original plan, you can again go back to the time and circumstances under which you structured the portfolio and see if anything has altered which would now permit you to include the new investment in your portfolio. Once again I repeat – this is your plan. It must be meaningful and relevant in light of your goals and investor personality.

And finally, should you decide at some point to engage a professional financial planner or investment advisor, you will both welcome a written statement as a point of reference for intention and a benchmark for performance.

Okay. We have gone through all four levels of the pyramid, spelling out your personal philosophy, setting objectives, determining asset allocation and selecting appropriate securities. Let us now do a quick review of the steps followed in designing your strategy and portfolio.

Level I – Investment Philosophy

Through a process of determining your personal *risk tolerance* and investor *personality,* you carry out one of the mandatory requirements for anyone giving investment advice, that is to "know the client." Since you are the client, it is imperative that you "know yourself."

Level II – Investment Objective

Deciding whether your priority should be *growth, income* or *liquidity* or some combination of all three is the second step in getting to "know yourself." This basic decision usually reflects your stage in life and therefore is influenced by age, career, family situation and financial planning objectives.

Level III – Asset Allocation

Considering the objectives set for yourself, what would be the best allocation of your assets into the three major categories of *cash, debt* or *equities?* The weightings will be largely determined by the level of risk you are willing to assume, which will then set an upper limit on the rate of return you can realistically expect from your portfolio.

Level IV – Security Selection

All assets that you might own or wish to own should be considered within their respective asset classes. Expected return and risk can be quantified to the extent that good information is available about the individual holdings. Diversification among well-chosen investments can yield a higher rate of return overall with less risk.

Summary

- *There is far more to the power of diversification than simply spreading your assets over a number of investments to reduce risk.*
- *By combining assets with different patterns of return, it is possible to achieve a higher rate of return without increasing risk.*

Chapter Ten:

Implementing Your Strategy

KEEP ONLY THOSE ASSETS YOU WOULD
BUY TODAY IF YOU DID NOT ALREADY OWN THEM;
SELL EVERYTHING ELSE.

You now have a completed Investment Statement which tells you *what* to do as far as putting together an appropriate investment portfolio. The next question is *how* do you go about actually implementing the decisions you have made? Obviously, if you were starting from scratch with only cash holdings which you were now going to diversify among the assets you had chosen, the task would be much simpler than if you had a collage of existing investments to try to incorporate into your plan.

Well if having a portfolio composed entirely of cash would make life easier, why don't we assume that is exactly what you have. You begin by *theoretically* converting all your existing assets to cash and seeing how much that adds up to. You can then compare where you *are* with where you *want to be*. Here is an example:

Current Portfolio

Asset	Asset Class	Dollar Value	% of Portfolio
Bank Account	Cash	$ 5,000	5%
Money Market Fund	Cash	$10,000	10%
Canada Savings Bond	Cash	$10,000	10%
Total of Asset Class		$25,000	25%
G.I.C. (5 Yr)	Debt	$20,000	20%
Company pension	Debt	$40,000	40%
Total of Asset Class		$60,000	60%
Shares in XYZ Ltd.	Equity	$10,000	10%
Growth Fund	Equity	$ 5,000	5%
Total of Asset Class		$15,000	15%

So this portfolio is comprised of:

Cash	$ 25,000	25%
Debt	60,000	60%
Equity	15,000	15%
Total	$100,000	100%

But let's suppose your desired allocation is:

Cash	$ 20,000	20%
Debt	40,000	40%
Equity	40,000	40%
Total	$100,000	100%

To get from where you are to where you want to be, you must somehow reduce the cash holding by $5,000 and the debt portion by $20,000, then shift the combined amount of $25,000 from those two asset classes to your equity component. Sounds simple enough, doesn't it? You could just cash in your GIC for $20,000, take $5,000 out of your money market fund and buy $25,000 worth of stocks. Right? Well... maybe not. A number of questions have to be answered first.

Timing of Portfolio Adjustments

From a psychological perspective, there are two sides to the argument as to *how quickly* transition to a new asset allocation should take place. On one side are those who might, for example, say, "Listen, I've gone through all this work; I know what I want to do so let's get on with it." The counterpoint to that is, "I agree with the plan I've outlined, but I would like to implement it over a period of time so I can gradually get used to the idea of having almost half of my portfolio in equity-type investments which fluctuate."

Dollar Cost Averaging

Both approaches are valid. If the new mix you propose doesn't threaten your "peace of mind" too much, go for it right away. If, on the other hand, you think more along the lines of the latter, more cautious group, the best strategy may be a planned transfer, over a period of time, of equal amounts from one asset class to another. This approach is called "dollar cost averaging" and makes particular sense for re-allocations into the equity category. Following is an example of "dollar cost averaging" at work, assuming you wanted to move, say, $10,000 into an equity mutual fund. You could take as long as you like, within some obvious practical limits given the amount of money you wish to re-allocate. In this example, you might take five or even 10 months to complete the transfer by making your purchases in either $2,000 or $1,000 amounts. Here is a possible outcome of a five-month purchase plan:

Timing	Amount	Fund Unit Price	# Units Purchased
Month 1	$2,000	$5.00	400
Month 2	$2,000	$4.00	500
Month 3	$2,000	$3.33	600
Month 4	$2,000	$4.00	500
Month 5	$2,000	$5.00	400
Totals	$10,000		2,400

Average price per unit = $10,000 / 2,400 units = $4.17

By Month 5, you would own 2,400 units, for which you paid a total of $10,000. That averages out to be $4.17 per unit, which demonstrates the major advantage of "dollar cost averaging": by making regular purchases of equal amounts, you purchase more units when prices are low and fewer when they go up. In Month 1, for example, your $2,000 bought 400 units at $5.00 per unit. As the price fell through Months 2 and 3, the same dollar amount purchased more units. Conversely, as the price began to rise, your $2,000 bought fewer units. This works best for assets with fluctuating prices, such as common stocks. As you can see from our example, even though the unit value declined immediately after you started your scheduled buys and never recovered to a level any higher than the one at which you started, you still managed to make a profit. You now own 2,400 units at a current price of $5.00. That adds up to $12,000 or $2,000 more than you invested. Again, I have purposely chosen these numbers to make my point but the theory is valid as long as the value of the unit does not continue to decline indefinitely. Then it is simply a bad investment choice and no matter how many units you buy at any price, you will lose money.

There is a psychological value derived from "dollar cost averaging."

It becomes apparent if you think about the volatility which might occur *in the short run* with equity investments, where their return can be quite different from the long-term projections on which you built your plan. "Averaging into the market" will normally dampen volatility, making the shorter-term experience more like the longer-term expectation. A good "rule of thumb," therefore, might be, "the more volatile the target asset is – the more time you should take to get there." In some cases, it may take as long as a year or even two years to reach the desired asset allocation.

What About RRSPs?

Moving money into and out of a Registered Retirement Savings Plan is not as straightforward as transfers within non-RRSP assets because there are restrictions on annual contributions and tax penalties for withdrawal. However, in general it is quite permissible to re-allocate to a different asset class as long as you remain under the RRSP umbrella. For example, you could transfer from your trust company RRSP which might be invested in a Term Deposit to an RRSP-qualified stock mutual fund, or vice versa. Properly documented, there would be no adverse tax effect as a result of that transaction. It is beyond the scope of this book to comment at length on *financial planning* strategies employing Registered Retirement Savings Plans. There are several excellent books available on that topic and once again my experience is that a knowledgeable financial advisor can assist enormously in this area. I will, however, make a couple of suggestions from an *investment* strategy viewpoint.

Although, for most people, RRSPs will be part of their longer-term strategy, they may not be the ideal place for long-term investments, such as equities. RRSPs are the most valuable tax concession available to Canadians. However, to derive maximum tax-deferral benefit you will want to shelter, within your RRSP, investments that generate the most taxable income – and that may not be your equity holdings. As I briefly commented back in Chapter 5, our tax regulations provide preferential treatment to investments that generate capital gains as compared to those that yield interest. This is accomplished by only taxing 75 percent of capital gains. The following table illustrates the relative tax position of investments in the three basic asset classes. Note that rates vary among provinces and this table is a simplified approximation. Again, good professional advisors can really earn their keep when it comes to something as complex as the Income Tax Act.

Tax Rates on Investment Income

Taxable Income	to $30,000	$30,000-$60,000	Top Rate
Interest	27%	42%	52%
Dividends	7%	25%	35%
Capital Gains	20%	31%	39%

So if you are not normally going to put equities into your RRSP, what are you going to include? As stated already, look first to those assets attracting the highest level of tax, which are most likely to be the interest-generating investments found in the *debt* category. Of course, you will also be earning interest on the *cash* component of your portfolio, but if the assets contained there are to serve their purpose as a source of liquid funds, you will not likely want to restrict access to them, which the tax consequences of a withdrawal from an RRSP might do. So your RRSP will largely be funded by your *debt* assets, such as GICs, term deposits, mortgages, bonds and so on.

The procedure for allocating assets to your RRSP is a two step one. First, make all of your asset allocation decisions as if there was no such thing as an RRSP. Tax considerations should always come second to sound investment strategy. Next, look at the specific investments you have chosen to have in your portfolio and pick out the one that attracts the highest rate of tax for each dollar invested. That is the investment that should go into your RRSP first. If you use all that particular asset and there is still room in your RRSP for additional contributions, choose the investment that attracts the next highest rate of tax. Keep repeating the process until the RRSP is fully invested.

And How About Pension Plans?

There is a tendency to ignore our pension plans in putting together an investment strategy because we assume there is little we can do to influence their performance and, in many cases, involvement in them is obligatory as an employee. However, if you are a member of a pension plan, scrutinize the plan to determine the specific investments *within* it so that you can allocate the value of the plan to its rightful asset class. If, for example, your pension is largely invested in Government of Canada Bonds, you will want to include it in your *debt* allocation; mostly blue-chip Canadian stocks, obviously an *equity* asset and so on. Then you can direct the money over which you *do* have control to balance the portfolio toward your intended allocation.

The same sort of considerations should be given to any other asset over which there is some limit to your ability to deal with it directly. Shares in your company, trust funds or deferred compensation would be additional examples.

Dealing with the Assets You Don't Want Anymore

One of the challenges you may face in making the transition from an existing portfolio structure to the newly desired one is what to do with assets you already own that don't fit into the revamped portfolio. This is a particular problem if today they are not worth what you paid for them. In other words, you have lost money on them but you are still holding them, waiting for the price to come back up. Somehow we convince ourselves in these situations that we haven't really lost the money until we actually sell the asset – the old "paper loss" theory. Well guess what? If that piece of real estate or stock has a current value lower than what you paid for it, you have lost money!

So what do you do about it? Obviously, you are not going to sell everything that has declined in value because, presumably, some of it does have potential to not only regain what it lost, but also add some profit. You might solve the dilemma by asking yourself this question: *"If I did not own this asset today, would I buy it?"*

If you can honestly answer that question with a "Yes," then, assuming the asset is appropriate for your target portfolio, hang on to it. On the other hand, if your response is something like, "Heck no! This thing is a dog... as soon as it gets back up to what I paid for it, I'm outta here," sell it now!

The converse also applies, when you have an asset that has increased substantially in value as you have owned it but doesn't fit in the new port-folio structure. A frequently encountered example of this is common stocks, perhaps even your company shares, that, when considered in the context of your new asset allocation, result in your having too much equity exposure in your portfolio overall. The question to ask yourself in this situation is, *"If I didn't own this asset today, would I buy it?"* Sound familiar?

If your answer is, "No way... it isn't worth today's price," sell it! You may have to delay the sale for a period of time or structure the disposal in a certain way to minimize the tax consequences, but in the case of an inappropriate asset, the general rule is *keep only those assets you would buy today if you did not already own them; sell everything else.*

Rebalancing the Portfolio

I have made the point several times that the asset-allocation decisions you make initially are not chiseled in stone – they can be changed at any time and, indeed, should be re-examined on a regular basis. In particular, if your personality as you defined it back in Chapter 6 tends towards the "passive" side of the Involvement line, you might think it less important to review your program once it is set up. That is because many investors equate a passive approach with a "buy and hold" strategy. In fact, those investors who want to be less involved in the investment process are often the ones who need to be most conscious of shifting asset allocations which may, over time, cease to reflect their risk tolerance. Let me expand a little more on this very important point.

If, as we agreed earlier, equities will outperform all other assets in the long run, it is inevitable that, over an extended time horizon, the equity portion of your portfolio will grow at a faster rate than the debt or cash components. Therefore, the equity side, if left unchanged, will gradually represent more and more of your total holdings. Here is a simple example of a portfolio that starts off with one half of its assets combined in the cash and debt classes and the other half in equities.

Asset Class	Initial Value	% of Portfolio	Growth Rate	Value in 5 Years	% of Portfolio
Cash	$ 20,000	20%	7%	$ 28,051	17%
Debt	$ 30,000	30%	8%	$ 44,080	28%
Equity	$ 50,000	50%	12%	$ 88,110	55%
Totals	$100,000	100%		$160,241	100%

At the end of five years, the combined cash and debt holdings fell from 50 percent to 45 percent of the total while the equity class increased from 50 percent to 55 percent of the overall portfolio. You may argue that such a small difference doesn't really matter, and you could be absolutely correct — if the slight increase in risk, from having 50 percent of your portfolio in equities to having 55 percent is still within your comfort zone. However, this example assumed normal expected rates of growth for the three asset classes. What if, in the space of five years, you experienced some unusual market conditions? Here is an example in which the equity market has a higher-than-expected return.

Equity Market Up

Asset Class	Initial Value	% of Portfolio	Growth Rate	Value in 5 Years	% of Portfolio
Cash	$ 20,000	20%	7%	$28,051	14%
Debt	$ 30,000	30%	8%	$ 44,080	22%
Equity	$ 50,000	50%	20%	$124,415	64%
Totals	$100,000	100%		$196,546	100%

Under this scenario, the equity of your portfolio would have jumped from one-half to almost two-thirds of the total — *while your time horizon decreased by five years.* That may still be acceptable to you — having the potential volatility increase simultaneously with the shrinking of the time horizon, provided your risk tolerance has expanded over that same period. If it hasn't, however, you will want to "rebalance" the portfolio. How do you rebalance? You pretend you are Robin Hood by stealing from the rich to give to the poor, that is, you take from the best-performing asset and give to the underperforming ones, like this:

Asset Class	Current %	Current Value	Desired %	Target Value	Difference	Action
Cash	14%	$ 28,051	20%	$39,309	$11,258	Buy
Debt	22%	$ 44,080	30%	$ 58,964	$14,844	Buy
	36%	$ 72,131	50%	$ 98,273	$26,142	
Equity	64%	$124,415	50%	$ 98,273	$26,142	Sell
	100%	$196,546	100%	$196,546		

The specifics of this example are that you should sell $26,142 worth of your best performing holdings, which were equities, to buy more cash and debt investments, prorating the purchase of each to return the portfolio to the balance you desire. Psychologically, this can be a very difficult thing to do if you have had an experience like the example above. I'm telling you to sell off the asset that has given you the best return to buy more of the ones that have not performed as well. But if you want to maintain the risk profile of your portfolio, that is exactly what you must do! And of course the theory also works the other way around: when the equity portion of the portfolio has fallen below its initial allocation, you have to sell some of the cash and debt assets to buy more equities. Otherwise, the inflation-fighting potential of your portfolio will be curtailed.

The other major advantage of the rebalancing tactic is that it disciplines us to adhere to one of the key tenets of successful investing, that is "buy low – sell high." Rebalancing a portfolio on a periodic basis automatically forces us to do that.

I suggested earlier that investors who tend towards the "passive" personality are the ones who should be on guard the most against a shifting risk profile of their portfolio. For those who are more "active" in their investment management, the theory still applies, of course, and particularly if some degree of "timing the market" is being practised. If you are that kind of investor, I would recommend that you set ranges for the amount you wish to have in each asset grouping, for example, 10-20 percent in cash, 20-50 percent in debt and 40-70 percent in equities. This will assure that a minimum is always kept in each class and yet provide flexibility to overweight or underweight any category as conditions change and one class becomes more or less attractive. I listed some suggested weightings (by age) back in Chapter 8.

When to Rebalance

As we were developing our Investment Statement, I made the comment that any change on the pyramid would automatically require a review of all higher levels, that is, a change of *Philosophy* (I) should prompt you to re-examine your *Objectives* (II), *Asset Allocation* (III) and *Security Selection* (IV) to see if they are still appropriate. Altering your *Objectives* (II) would necessitate a look at your *Asset Allocation* (III) and *Security Selection* (IV) and so on. Obviously, then, just about any change in your thinking or the assumptions on which you based your decisions about portfolio structure should lead you to at least looking at the asset allocation. Alternatively, I believe that an annual review is a good idea.

Measuring Performance

As you review the asset allocation on a regular basis, you'll also want to determine how well the portfolio you have put in place is doing for you. Obviously, you can easily measure the absolute return simply by adding up the present value of all your assets and comparing that to the value at the start of the period. But to gauge the effectiveness of your asset allocation you should compare your actual results with the expected returns and volatility you spelled out in Level IV of your Investment Statement. If your target was, say, 12 percent average return with a "fluctuation factor" of ±10 percent and the actual results are -30 percent or + 30 percent, try to determine the reason. Is the variance just a short term aberration or was something grossly over- or under-estimated from the beginning?

Obviously, you can't be too quick to judge or make changes because short-term volatility is to be expected. However, as an additional measure, compare the performance of the specific securities you have chosen against benchmarks for the asset classes. For example, if the equity component of your portfolio is represented by growth mutual funds invested in Canada, plot their return against the Toronto Stock Exchange (TSE 300) Index results; U.S. stocks can be compared to the Standard & Poor (S & P 500) Index and so on. The financial newspapers regularly publish statistics on the returns of various investments, especially interest yields on T-Bills, bonds and mortgages, stock market returns and mutual fund performance, so you can make relatively accurate comparisons if your portfolio is comprised of those assets. The more esoteric your investment choices are, however, the more difficult it will be to find a relevant benchmark, so you will have to rely on your Investment Statement. There is nothing wrong with that – if your portfolio results are meeting your needs and expectations, it doesn't matter very much how well it is doing compared to an alternative allocation. *The long-term goal of this process is to achieve your financial objectives, not necessarily to "beat the market."*

Getting Money Out of the Portfolio

If you are one of the millions of Canadians who have had the "don't put all your eggs in one basket" advice repeated to you over and over again, you have probably also been warned to "never spend the principal." The intention of this latter counsel is sound – if you can live off the interest earnings from your investments, you will never run out of money. The problem is that while your income may continue forever, the ability of that income to buy you the goods and services you want or need may well be deteriorating. Obviously, we are talking about the ravages of inflation. Back in Chapter 2, I referred to inflation as a "double demon" because it has two serious ramifications for investors. First, it destroys accumulated wealth and secondly, it reduces the purchasing power of income. The following chart illustrates both dangers.

Years	Value of Capital (@ 6% inflation)	Income (@ 8% return)
Now	$500,000	$40,000
12	$250,000	$20,000
24	$125,000	$10,000
36	$ 62,500	$ 5,000

Let's imagine for a moment that you are retiring, in good health, at, say, age 60. Your normal life expectancy would be another twenty to twenty-five years. Let's also suppose that you have an accumulated investment portfolio of $500,000 and you want to use it to provide you with the maximum amount of income it can. However, because your parents admonished you to "never spend the principal" you believe you must re-allocate your portfolio to be entirely invested in assets that generate regular interest payments in order to maximize the income you can receive without tapping into the capital. Thinking of the three representative investments we have used throughout this book as examples, you rightfully conclude that long-term government bonds have the highest expected interest return, about eight percent. Invested entirely in bonds, then, your $500,000 would provide $40,000 of interest income in the first year. Now look twelve years down the road to age 72. If, during the intervening years, inflation was a modest six percent, you would see the value of your capital fall, in terms of today's worth, to about half – $250,000. Remember the "Rule of 72"? (Divide 72 by the inflation rate and you will know approximately the number of years it takes for capital values to be cut in half.)

More important, however, is the impact on income. As a retiree attempting to live on interest only, you see the *purchasing power* of your income fall by 50 percent as well, to $20,000, *even though you were able to earn a return greater than the rate of inflation!* If you were fortunate enough to survive another twelve years to age 84, which is becoming increasingly likely, given advances in medical technology, you would have the pleasure of seeing your income cut in half again, to the equivalent of $10,000. If you made it all the way to age 96, you would be trying to get by on an income with a purchasing power of only $5,000!

What's more, by converting all your assets into interest generating ones, you automatically lower the overall expected return from your portfolio as you eliminate all the higher performing equity investments. It has been said several times before but warrants repeating here: *portfolios with long time horizons need equities in them* and someone retiring at age 60 certainly has a time horizon sufficiently long for it to be appropriate to include equities. In setting up your portfolio to provide income, you must think in terms of total return, which includes dividends and capital gains from equities, interest and perhaps some capital gains from debt-type assets as well as the interest produced by cash holdings. It is better to spend a little principal from a portfolio with a higher total return than to design one with maximum "interest only" income but lower overall yield.

The next big question in your mind should be, "If I am going to spend part of the principal, how much can I take out of my portfolio and still be assured that I will never run out of money?" Regrettably, there is no simple answer to that because no one knows how long he or she is going to live and, thus, how long the money has to last. Obviously, too large a withdrawal can have devastating effects. Even with only modest levels of persistent inflation, the purchasing power of a portfolio can significantly erode over time if too much of its average total return is used to meet expenditures.

The ideal way to preserve purchasing power is to *limit your withdrawals from the portfolio to the earnings in excess of the rate of inflation*. For example, if your portfolio earns 12 percent and inflation is five percent, you should only withdraw the difference, which is seven percent. In real life, this rule might prove to be a real challenge if the difference between the portfolio return and inflation does not result in sufficient income. As the years passed, you *would* be able to increase the actual dollar amount withdrawn annually because the total value of the portfolio would rise each year by the net amount allowed for inflation, but even that may not be adequate to meet your needs. Try as best you can, however, to get by on something less than the total return so that there is at least a partial hedge against inflation. Once more, here is where a good financial planner can assist in coordinating all your government and employee benefits with your personal retirement income sources. Below is a table that illustrates the withdrawal strategy just described assuming an average 10 percent income yield and a four percent allowance for inflation.

Year	Beginning Value	Income @ 10%	Inflation @ 4%	Net Income	Portfolio Balance
1	$200,000	$20,000	$8,000	$12,000	$208,000
2	208,000	20,800	8,300	12,500	216,300
3	216,300	21,600	8,600	13,000	224,900
4	224,900	22,500	9,000	13,500	233,900
5	233,900	23,400	9,400	14,000	243,300

As you can see, the income gradually grew over the five-year period as did the size of the portfolio. This example assumes a constant rate of return and inflation. You and I know, however, that the real world of investing is more volatile and adhering to the rule of withdrawing only the excess after inflation may be impossible. There could, in fact, be years when your income would decline unless you took out a little more than the net return. Hopefully, of course, there will also be times when the portfolio will yield quite a bit more than what you need to offset increases in the cost of living. In either instance, the advice is the same: try to avoid withdrawing all of the income as it is earned.

Summary

- *Begin by theoretically converting all your existing assets to cash and then comparing where you are with where you want to be.*
- *"Dollar cost averaging" is a planned transfer, over a period of time, of equal amounts from one asset class to another. It makes particular sense for re-allocations into the equity category.*
- *Make all of your asset allocation decisions as if there was no such thing as an RRSP and put the assets which attract the highest rate of tax for each dollar invested into your RRSP first.*
- *Keep only those assets you would buy today if you did not already own them; sell everything else.*
- *Rebalancing a portfolio on a periodic basis automatically forces us to "buy low – sell high."*
- *The long-term goal of asset allocation is to achieve your financial objectives, not necessarily to "beat the market."*
- *It is better to spend a little principal from a portfolio with a higher total return than to design one with maximum "interest only" income but lower overall yield.*
- *Limit your withdrawals from the portfolio to the earnings in excess of the rate of inflation.*

So there you have it. We have gone the complete route now, from designing a portfolio and adjusting it over time as conditions change to converting the accumulated wealth into income. It hasn't been such a bad experience, has it? And now, just as we did at the end of Part I, let's review what we have covered in the past few chapters.

The primary task was the development of the Investment Statement in four parts:

Level I – Investment Philosophy is a function of *risk tolerance* and *personality*. Most Canadians are relatively low-risk investors and their personalities can be identified, in a general way, by measuring how *spontaneous* they are and to what extent they want to be *involved* in the investment decision-making process. By combining these two tendencies, we identified four distinct investor behaviour patterns: the *Active Market Timer,* the *Passive Market Timer,* the *Active Money Manager* and the *Passive Money Manager.* We know there are differences among them so you were asked to categorize yourself, with the knowledge that there is no right or wrong way to behave because there are successful investors who display each of the four personalities.

Level II – Setting Objectives required you to think about whether you want your investments to *grow* in value, provide an *income* or be available as a *liquid* source of cash for emergencies or opportunities. Your objectives will change over time as life events shape your attitudes and priorities; your portfolio, however, will probably always be structured with assets that address all three objectives.

We also learned that, given reasonable assumptions about rates of return, your portfolio might be too small to achieve all your goals and, while it may be possible to combine investments with a cumulative expected return that will meet your objectives, chances are that the risk associated with such a portfolio will be too high. Consequently, it is usually better to concentrate on designing a portfolio that is within your risk tolerance rather than attempting to achieve a target rate of return. Once your "comfort zone" is established, it automatically sets an upper limit on the long-term rate of return you can expect from your portfolio. If that return won't achieve all your objectives, you will have to scale them down or expand your risk tolerance so you can include assets with higher expected returns. Alternatively, you must be prepared to commit more money to your investment program. In many situations, a combination of all three actions – reducing objectives, expanding your "comfort zone" and increasing the dollar amount of your investment – will be required.

Level III – Asset Allocation builds on the philosophy and objective-setting phases by marrying certain asset classes with specific objectives. The basic allocation decision is made by answering the question, *"Given my personal philosophy and my objectives, what percentage of my assets should be allocated to cash, what percentage to debt and what percentage to equity?"*

You learned how to calculate expected return and expected risk for a traditional portfolio and how to make the trade-off between risk and reward by shifting weightings of the various assets within your portfolio, increasing the equity portion if a higher rate of return was the objective or boosting up the cash and debt components if your objective was to reduce volatility.

Level IV – Selecting Securities is the top of our investment pyramid and as such it is the smallest piece. That is quite appropriate because if each of the previous steps has been carefully done, actually selecting the specific securities to include in your portfolio is the easiest part of the entire exercise. It becomes a simple matter of choosing investments that combine to yield a rate of return that meets your needs yet have a cumulative fluctuation factor with which you can live. We saw that by broadly diversifying your portfolio among a number of assets with different risk/reward characteristics, you can simultaneously reduce volatility and increase total return.

The culmination of the four-step process is an Investment Statement that accurately describes who you are as an investor, what your goals are, how you are going to achieve them and the anticipated outcome from your portfolio structure. This statement will serve as a benchmark for performance and as a reference point for evaluating new investment opportunities as they come along. It is not, though, a "forever" thing – you must review your investment strategies regularly and amend them to meet your evolving needs.

And now I ask you to recall the introduction to this book in which I said that I am of the very strong belief that *mutual funds* are the best investment choice for most of us – whether we are experienced, sophisticated investors or just starting out in our wealth accumulation programs. Everything that we have discussed about risk management, matching investments to objectives, allocating assets, selecting securities and rebalancing portfolios can be accomplished through the use of mutual funds. They are the most all-encompassing investment available. Part III of this book examines mutual funds, not by describing how they work from a technical viewpoint but rather by considering how they fit with the theories and can be applied to the procedures we have developed throughout Part I and Part II. Even though you may be quite familiar with the mutual fund concept, I encourage you to join me in Part III to see how it can be so readily integrated into your asset allocation strategy.

Chapter Eleven:
Mutual Funds

MUTUAL FUNDS ARE THE BEST INVESTMENT CHOICE
FOR MOST CANADIANS AND REPRESENT THE FASTEST GROWING
SEGMENT OF THE FINANCIAL SERVICES INDUSTRY.

Mutual funds are, in my opinion, the best investment choice for most Canadians and apparently, an increasing number of investors share that opinion because today they represent the fastest growing segment of the financial services industry. Sales have skyrocketed over the past ten years and Canadian mutual fund managers now look after more than $125 billion of our money. That is an increase of about 3000 percent since the mid-1980s and some forecasts put the size of the industry at $300 billion by the year 2000. That pace of sales growth and the large number of books available that describe in detail all the technicalities of mutual funds suggest to me that many people are familiar with mutual funds. Therefore, I am not going to spend very much time discussing how they work but rather, I will try to explain why they have such appeal. I'll describe their features, advantages and benefits and then show how mutual funds can be used in the development of your Investment Statement.

Features

Sometimes also referred to as "investment funds" (or "unit trusts" in other parts of the world), mutual funds developed from three basic investment strategies:

a) Pooling of assets,

b) Diversification and

c) Professional management.

Let's follow the evolution from the first of these through to the last with a simple example.

Pooling of Assets

Suppose that you and I each had $10,000 to invest. We know from some reading we've done that, over the long term, stocks will deliver greater returns than cash- or debt-type investments, so we decide to purchase shares in publicly traded companies. Before we select which stocks to buy, however, we both do a little research. You, because you have a more *active* investor personality, have been studying all the financial newspapers and have even requested the annual reports of a couple of companies that caught your attention. I, on the other hand, being more *passively* inclined, have simply been asking for recommendations from a few people who I know are experienced investors.

The result of our individual research is that you decide to buy 2,000 shares of ABC Ltd., a fast-growing computer software company, at $5.00 per share and I settle on XYZ Inc., a large, well-established conglomerate, currently trading at $100.00 a share, so I get 100 shares for my $10,000 investment. Periodically, we play golf together and inevitably, the conversation turns to our investments with each of us expounding on the wise choice we made. (Remember our need for "bragging rights"?) You talk about the excitement of owning ABC Ltd. Its price is now $6.50 per share, an increase of 30 percent – but it has also

174

dropped to as low as $4.00 while you've owned it. The long-term prospects remain bright but the stock does have a history of high price volatility so you could be in for a bit of a wild ride along the way. By comparison, my experience with XYZ Inc. has been rather boring. Its price has never fallen below what I paid for it and in fact, it has risen unceremoniously to $110.00 per share – an increase of 10 percent. I don't think about it very often and assume it will continue to perform in a similar manner for many years to come.

Over a post-game refreshment in the clubhouse one day, we quietly admit that we wouldn't mind if our individual investments exhibited more of the characteristics of the other's, that is, you would welcome some of the stability of my XYZ Inc. and I certainly wouldn't be unhappy with a higher return, such as you have experienced with ABC Ltd. We agree that the easiest way to combine the lower volatility of XYZ Inc. with the superior returns of ABC Ltd. is for each of us to own shares of both companies. There are two ways to accomplish this. I could sell some of my XYZ Inc. and use the proceeds to buy shares of ABC Ltd. You, of course, would do the reverse. Instead, we decide to form a simple partnership with each of us contributing our respective holdings and sharing, on a pro rata basis, in the profits. In other words, we *pool our assets* so that we *jointly* now own 2,000 shares of ABC Ltd. and 100 shares of XYZ Inc. (For simplicity, I will ignore the relative profits earned to this point.)

By doing this, we have achieved two things. First, we have created a larger capital base with which to work. If, at some point down the road, we decide to sell our holdings in ABC Ltd. and XYZ Inc. in favour of buying something else, we will, presumably, have about twice as much money to reinvest. This will give us much more flexibility in choosing alternate investments because some of the other opportunities we might examine may only be available to us if we have a minimum amount of cash to commit. For example, if we decided to abandon stocks altogether and buy real estate, the more money we had in total, the greater the choice of properties we could consider.

Diversification

The second and most important consequence of pooling our assets is that we get to enjoy the power of *diversification*. I have already described at length the tremendous benefit that can be derived by combining two or more assets with different performance characteristics. In our example, we would expect that if we put one half of the portfolio into ABC Ltd. and the other half into XYZ Inc., the new "two-stock" portfolio will have a more consistent return than one that just contained ABC Ltd. and a higher yield than one holding XYZ Inc. exclusively. As our portfolio grows and we are able to include additional, carefully chosen investments, we can actually increase total return within a given risk level or alternatively, maintain the same expected return while lowering the overall risk profile. That is exactly what mutual funds do – they automatically diversify your investment dollars over a larger number of assets than you could likely purchase on your own. As I am writing this, if you had $10,000 to invest in the Canadian stock market, you could buy any of the following:

1,000,000 shares – Lasir Gold, or
500,000 shares – Artistic Photography, or
100,000 shares – Thunder Engines, or
10,000 shares – Solar Pharmaceutical, or
4,000 shares – Air Canada, or
1,000 shares – Scott's Hospitality, or
400 shares – Bell Canada, or
250 shares – Magna International, or
150 shares – IBM.

By comparison, if you invested in a well-known Canadian equity mutual fund, your same $10,000, as part of a large pool of investors' money, would purchase this diversified portfolio:

Canadian Equity Securities

AGRA Industries Limited, Class B	$ 30
Alcan Aluminum Limited	510
Alias Research Inc.	40
Bank of Montreal	230
CAE Industries Ltd.	250
Canfor Corporation	310
CCL Industries Inc., Class B	40
Co-Steel Inc.	170
Devtek Corporation, Class A	20
Dylex Limited, Class A Preferred	17
Emco Limited	20
Federal Industries Ltd., Class A	20
Finning Ltd.	250
Imperial Oil Limited	330
Inco Limited	440
Inter-City Products Corporation	70
Lawson Mardon Group Limited, Class A	200
LSI Logic Corporation of Canada, Inc.	30
Metall Mining Corporation	50
Nova Corporation of Alberta	310
Nowsco Well Service Ltd.	40
Parkland Industries Ltd.	10
Potash Corporation of Saskatchewan Inc.	170
Reed Stenhouse Companies Limited, Class 1 Special	30
Renaissance Energy Ltd.	310
Rogers Communication Inc., Class B	320
The Royal Bank of Canada	430
Saskatchewan Oil & Gas Corporation	30
Scheinder Corporation, Class A	60
Scott's Hospitality Inc.	280
SHL Systemhouse Inc.	190
Southam Inc.	180

Teck Corporation, Class B	410
Toromont Industries	40
The Toronto Dominion Bank	210
The Toronto Sun Publishing Corporation	130
Trimac Limited	230
Unican Security Systems Ltd., Class A	30
Unican Security Systems Ltd., Class B	50
Univa Inc.	220
	67.8%

Foreign Equity Securities

Beckman Instruments Inc.	$ 160
Ecolab Inc.	190
Manpower, Inc.	300
MCI Communications Corporation	370
Paramount Communications Inc.	290
Raychem Corporation	380
Tandy Corporation	320
	20.1%
	87.9%

Bonds and Convertible Debentures

Emco Limited, Conv. Deb.	
• 7.25%, April 30, 2002	$ 10
Government of Canada	
• 10.00%, March 01, 1995	50
Government of Canada	
• 8.5%, April 01, 2002	140
Government of Canada	
• 11.00%, June 01, 2009	20
Government of Canada	
•9.75%, June 01, 2021	50
Ontario Hydro • 8.25%, July 21, 1996	50
Parkland Industries, Ltd., Conv. Deb.	

• 9.00%, April 30, 1999	10
Province of Saskatchewan	
• 12.25%, June 05, 1995	70
	4.0%
	91.9%
Short-term investments and other assets (net)	8.1%
Net Assets	100%

It is easy to see that a single purchase of a mutual fund can immediately create a very broadly diversified portfolio. Let's go on.

Professional Management

So far we have looked at two of the key features of mutual funds: the pooling of assets and diversification. To explore the third one, professional management, let us return to the golf club where you and I are discussing our joint investment holdings. As we do so, either on the course itself or at the "19th Hole," chances are that a few of our golfing buddies will overhear some of the conversation and it won't be very long before they are offering suggestions as to good investment opportunities. Some of them might even want to join us in our pooling arrangement and before we know it, we could have a small investment club with each member contributing ideas and cash to buy more investments on a shared basis. As the number of people and the amount of money increases, we'll probably want to meet more formally from time to time, to make decisions about which stocks to buy or sell and to distribute any profits. We may also have to find a volunteer to account for the assets of the club, negotiate commissions with brokers and deal with the paperwork that comes from buying and selling stocks. Periodically, we could even invite a specialist to one of our gatherings to educate us on specific investments or to provide us with research to aid in our decision making.

If we follow the natural life cycle of a group of investors such as I have just described, the day will come when someone stands up at one of the meetings and says, "This thing has just gotten too big to continue in such an informal way. The paperwork has become a burden, we all have our own ideas about the investments we should be making and none of us has the time or skill to sort it all out in a way which can maximize return without exposing us to too much risk. I would like to propose that we hire a manager to look after all of these details. We can find a professional who has the *same philosophy* (remember? – risk tolerance + personality = philosophy) as we do, with a *good track record* in choosing stocks, *knowledge of the regulatory requirements* and the *administrative capability* to handle our affairs. I would be willing to pay that manager a small portion of our total assets as compensation." From statements such as those, the mutual fund manager is born!

Before we look more closely at the duties we expect them to perform, let me pause to differentiate between a couple of similar descriptive terms, specifically, "mutual fund manager" and "portfolio manager." They are occasionally used interchangeably but in fact are quite different. The mutual fund manager, according to my dictionary, provides all of the services associated with the marketing and administration of mutual funds, including sales, promotion, processing of transactions, distribution of information, ensuring regulatory compliance, accounting and reporting to unit-holders. In addition, *the mutual fund manager hires the portfolio manager* to study markets, set out portfolio strategies, buy and sell securities and maximize return for the level of risk that the investors expect, given the objectives stated in the fund's prospectus. Portfolio managers are also often referred to as "investment managers" because that is what they do – look after the investments, not the investors. That is not to say that they don't care about the investors because in fact, many portfolio managers are also shareholders in the management companies they represent. It is just that their focus is on the management of investors' money rather than the service aspect of the business.

The first responsibility of such a portfolio manager is to communicate his or her *investment philosophy* so that investors can decide if there is a match between their personal philosophy and that of the portfolio manager. Do they, for example, subscribe to the "market timing" school of thought or take a "money management" approach? Are they "value investors" who search for stocks with prices that appear to be below the actual value of the company? Or do they employ a "top down" strategy, first determining broad economic outlook by answering questions such as, "Is the country in an expansion or a contraction phase?" or "Are interest rates headed up or down?" or "What are the prospects for inflation?" and then selecting companies which they expect to perform the best under the anticipated economic conditions?

Once the philosophy is determined, the professional manager must develop an *investment strategy* that keeps the portfolio on a consistent track towards its objective which might be long-term capital appreciation for equity funds or above-average income with preservation of capital for bond funds or high short-term yield for money market funds. Then the manager must buy and sell assets to execute the strategy, keep account of all the transactions, handle investors' purchases and redemptions, distribute profits, issue tax statements and receipts, comply with the innumerable regulations and report to investors on a regular basis.

In Canada, there are about one hundred firms that provide the services I have described through various mutual funds. Choosing the ones that are appropriate for you can be somewhat daunting. I have alluded to some of the factors you should consider with respect to philosophy and objectives and I'll give you additional guidelines to follow in the next chapter. For now, however, the important message is that, in most cases, these organizations are better equipped to provide the level of professional expertise required for successful investing than we are individually. And what's more, they do it all at a most reasonable cost, typically about two percent of the dollar value of the assets they manage. That, in my opinion, is a real bargain when one considers the enormous responsibility and the infastructure and personnel needed to carry out the task.

Advantages

Let's move on to the advantages that mutual funds exhibit over many other investments. There is no particular priority to the following list. Mutual funds attract a wide range of investors who are drawn by different advantages.

Liquidity

Mutual funds can normally be redeemed for their cash value in the few days it takes to process the request and in practice, a number of companies can provide same-day emergency redemption, including electronic transfer of the proceeds to your bank. Mutual funds are not as liquid, therefore, as your savings account because you cannot typically walk into a local office or branch and withdraw the cash, although some fund companies do offer limited chequing privileges. However, you are able to access your money much more readily than you can with, say, any investment you might have in a mortgage, a limited partnership, a piece of real estate or your own company shares.

On the assumption that most Canadians will purchase publicly traded, open-end mutual funds (which are far and away the most popular), what is even more beneficial is the fact that there is a *guaranteed buyer!* That's what "open-end" implies. The mutual fund itself will always buy back the units you own, without question and with no argument as to how much they are going to pay you because the values of fund units are published daily in all major newspapers. On any morning that you wake up and decide to sell your mutual fund, you can look in *The Globe and Mail, The Financial Post* or, in many cities, your local newspaper for the daily unit value, call your broker or financial product specialist and know that your fund is disposed of at a known price.

In recent years, a new purchase arrangement called the "deferred sales charge" has become commonplace wherein there is no sales commission deducted from your deposits, but there is a fee for early redemption, usually within six to nine years of the initial purchase. This may affect the total proceeds you receive if you redeem your fund, but has nothing to do with the selling price. It is simply a commission similar to that which you would pay if you were selling many other investments, such as stocks, bonds, mortgages, real estate or works of art.

Diversification

A couple of pages back I showed the difference between what $10,000 would buy if you invested in a single stock and what you would own if you purchased a well-known Canadian mutual fund with the same dollar amount. That example clearly illustrated the diversification effect of investment funds but in fact, the advantage can be far more substantial. In his exceptionally good book Multifund Investing, *How To Build A High Performance Portfolio of Mutual Funds,* Michael Hirsch describes the "triple safety net" which comes with using a number of mutual funds to carry out your investment strategy. The first level of safety is the diversification within a single fund itself. Most equity funds, for example, will own anywhere from 40 to more than 100 stocks, depending on the size of the fund and its investment objective. Consequently, if stocks of firms in the retailing business, for example, aren't doing too well, the energy stocks might be and so on. Bond funds might hold 10 to 15 different issues; real estate funds may own 20 to 30 properties or more. The basic notion of diversification as a means of reducing volatility and increasing return can be found in a single mutual fund.

But what if, for example, the stock market is in a slump and equities in general aren't performing in a particularly exciting manner ? This is where the second line of defence comes into play. By owning mutual funds that invest in *more than one asset class,* you can extend the value of diversification even further. Why not have at least part of your portfolio made up of mutual funds that specialize in each of cash, debt and equity investments? in Canada, we at present have more than 800 different mutual funds available to individual investors. The breakdown, according to asset class is:

Cash	109 Funds
Debt	186 Funds
Equity	404 Funds
	699

In addition, there are more than 100 "balanced" funds which spread their investments over all three asset classes within the funds themselves. So it is quite possible to have a second level of diversification by constructing a portfolio with mutual funds that are not only diversified among assets but among asset *classes*.

The third "safety net" is put into place when you select mutual funds with different investment managers. As mentioned previously, there are approximately 100 mutual fund companies in Canada and many of them offer competing products. For example, at least 70 of those 100 firms offer an equity fund which specializes in Canadian stocks. Chances are that among 70 independent investment managers, there will be some difference of opinion as to how money should be invested at any particular moment. Some will believe that interest rates have further to fall and will include in their portfolios companies that typically profit from declines in interest rates. Others will think that rates have bottomed out and are set to rise. Consequently, they will look to invest in companies with good prospects under those conditions. Some who are more "market timing" oriented may anticipate a general downward movement in the stock market and will, therefore, increase the cash component of their portfolios to avoid having all their capital in the market as it declines and also to have money available to purchase stocks at the expected lower prices. The more fundamental money managers may feel that their mandate calls for them to always be invested in equities so they will look for companies that represent long-term value regardless of short term market fluctuations. All of these managers can be successful even though they have differing philosophies. So why not *diversify among managers* to minimize the risk that the single management firm you have chosen might be wrong from time to time? As Sir John Templeton, patriarch of the mutual fund industry, writes in his foreword to Roger Gibson's excellent book, *Asset Allocations: Balancing Financial Risk,* "To diversify your investments is clearly common sense so that those which produce more profits than expected will offset those which produce less. Even the best investment professional must expect that no more than two thirds of his decisions will prove to be above average in profits. Therefore, asset allocation and diversification are the foundation stones of successful, long-term investing." There is no "all-weather" manager who performs well under every market condition so diversifying among managers will give you, as Michael Hirsch describes it, "the combined yet independent expertise of a number of professionals."

Variety

I have already made the point that there are over 800 mutual funds available in Canada and that they cover the three basic asset classes. Closer examination, however, reveals that the diversity is even greater. We can tabulate the mutual funds available in Canada like this:

Asset Class	Fund Type	# Funds
Cash	Canadian Money Market	95
	International Money Market	14
Debt	Canadian Bond	104
	International Bond	27
	Mortgage	27
	Dividend	22
	Real Estate	6
Equity	Canadian	175
	International	131
	U.S.	77
	Specialty	21
Combined	Balanced/Asset Allocation	104
		803

These fund types can be defined even further. For example, about 72 percent of the 803 funds listed above fully qualify as RRSP investments. Some funds make monthly distributions of income; others do so quarterly or, most commonly, on an annual basis. The smallest fund has about $150,000 invested in it while the largest has more than $3.6 billion. Some have very low volatility and some very high. One-year rates of return range from +144 to -30 percent and 10-year compound average returns vary from more than 21 percent to less than three. About 80 of the 800 or so funds available have a front-end sales commission: 70 have a deferred sales charge arrangement; 276 can be purchased either way, that is, with an optional front-end or deferred sales charge and 375 are sold on a "no-load" basis. Most can be purchased under an automatic bank withdrawal agreement or with lump-sum deposits. Some restrict themselves to direct sales to members (and their families) of certain professional or trade associations whereas the best known funds are available through stock brokers, independent mutual fund salespeople, banks and trust companies, insurance agents and other "one-company" salespeople, as well as on a direct purchase basis by mail or telephone.

The number of options available to investors using mutual funds is enormous. You can choose funds representing each asset class or have someone else diversify among the classes for you by purchasing a balanced fund or a fund where the manager does the overall asset allocation. Your RRSP contribution can be made into a mutual fund and you can make regular deposits through your bank account to take advantage of "dollar cost averaging." If income is the objective, it can be received on a monthly, quarterly or annual basis. You can select funds with a history of providing the levels of return you need to meet your goals and a volatility factor that is within your comfort zone. Large, well-established funds with long-term track records of stable returns can be mixed with smaller, more aggressive choices to increase overall return potential. For total variety, mutual funds are difficult to match. They can be bought through just about every financial intermediary, in almost any amount, under numerous purchase arrangements and *there is a mutual fund to meet every financial objective.*

Full Time Management

The value of having a full-time, dedicated professional look after your portfolio can, perhaps, best be illustrated by recounting an experience I had a few years ago. One day, an elderly gentleman appeared at my office unexpectedly and asked for a few minutes of my time. At that stage of my career, I was working with a well-established mutual fund management company that had a very good long-term track record for its Canadian equity fund. The gentleman, whom I'll refer to as Mr. B., told me that he had been following the results of my firm's fund and wanted to invest some of his money in it. I had to tell him that our funds were distributed through brokers and independent mutual fund salespeople and therefore, it was a policy of our firm not to accept direct investments. I went on to say that I would, however, be happy to refer him to several good representatives from whom he could choose one who seemed best able to provide the level of expertise he required and with whom he felt a good rapport could be established. When he somewhat reluctantly agreed, I suggested that if he told me a little about his personal situation, I could narrow the list of potential advisors down to a few whose philosophies and methodologies were such that I thought they could accomodate his needs.

Here is Mr. B.'s story. He had been an employee of a national transportation firm for over 40 years, beginning as a yard helper and retiring at age 65 from a position as a department supervisor. His income, very modest at first, had risen steadily as he progressed through the firm but it had never been what one could call "generous." At this point, I will admit to you that I was taken back when Mr. B. next told me that, despite limitations on his disposable income, he had an investment portfolio that was worth $1.2 million! He went on to say, "Investing has been my hobby since I was a teenager; in fact, it has been an obsession with me. I have spent 20 to 30 hours a week for the past 50 years playing the stock and bond markets and managing my investments. As my portfolio has grown, I've had to dedicate more and more time to just keeping up with the paperwork and now, quite frankly, I'm a little tired. I still enjoy the thrill of analyzing companies, interest rate trends and such, but I'd like someone else to take on a large part of that responsibility for me. And I'm willing to pay them to do that." (Sound familiar?)

"What's more," Mr. B. went on to say, "my wife has never been too crazy about all the time I've spent with our investments rather than with the family. And certainly, should anything happen to me, she wouldn't have a clue about what to do with all the stocks and bonds and mortgages in the portfolio. So what I was hoping to do was to take $1 million of the $1.2 million total and put it into a few good mutual funds, to let the professionals manage it for me and for my wife if I'm not around.

The balance of $200,000 I intend to keep as my 'play money'. I will continue to do what I have been doing because I enjoy it, but I'll do so on a much smaller scale."

The happy conclusion to this story is that Mr. B. built a close relationship with a competent financial advisor who not only allocated the money among several good mutual funds but also assisted Mr. B. with his estate planning. Perhaps, however, the more telling sequel came to me a few weeks later when I was extolling the virtues of long-term investing in mutual funds to another, much young person. I was able to illustrate, with actual performance experience of a very popular common stock fund, how a $10,000 investment in 1954 would today be worth $2.1 million with all management fees accounted for and *the investor would not have had to even look at it since the day it was invested!* All the time that someone like Mr. B. devoted to managing his portfolio could be spent doing something else for personal enjoyment, family, faith, community or whatever. I understand that investing was Mr. B.'s passion and he got considerable psychic reward from the time and effort he employed in that activity and I know that $10,000 was a lot of money to start with in 1954, but the point is still valid - a professional manager is likely to be in a better position to do the things necessary for successful investing, leaving you free to spend your time on other, more personally appealing, pursuits. And chances are that you'll end up with a better-performing portfolio overall.

The other advantage to having professional managers on your side is that they are on the job full time. All of the myriad responsibilities of a mutual fund manager are carried out by a team of specially trained experts who do nothing else all day long but look after your money. Furthermore, they don't take phone calls! "So what?" you say? Let me ask you, "How many 'hot investment tips' have you received and how many of them turned out as promised?" I bet not many have come even close to the claims the tipster made. Well, professional portfolio managers don't act on "hot tips." They rely on sophisticated research, a massive data bank, specialist advisors and a proven methodology for making intelligent, considered investment decisions. How can we possibly hope to outperform them by ourselves?

Flexibility

I have already mentioned several times the considerable flexibility of investment options available through the use of mutual funds. Let me expand a little more on some of the key ones with an example. How would you react if you were an investment advisor and one of your clients made the following request?

"I'd like to open an investment account so that I can begin to accumulate wealth in an organized way. My intention is to set aside, say, $500 a month for the next twenty years. And here's what I'd like you, my friendly advisor, to do for me. Each month, please automatically withdraw the $500 from my bank account because I don't want to have to send you a cheque every four weeks or so. However, from time to time, I may want to stop and subsequently re-start the withdrawals or change the amount. I'll try to give you a couple of weeks notice but I'm not sure when or even if I will want to make that change. Periodically, I may drop in a few extra bucks in a lump sum or alternatively, I may have to dip into my account on occasion for a little cash. I'd like one-third of my investment to go into income producing assets such as bonds or mortgages for my RSP, 25 percent into Canadian blue chip stocks, $100 a month into Japanese securities and the balance into some sort of cash account with interest calculated daily and credited to my account on a monthly basis. I'll take a look at the asset mix and the results every six months or so and may want to shift some of my holdings from one investment to another. I don't mind paying your commission up front on the bond or mortgage purchases; however, the current yields on cash-type investments are so low, I'd rather not pay any commission at all on those. It is likely that I will always have a substantial portion of my portfolio in equities so I'd like to give you my money with no up-front fee but you can charge me if I withdraw in the next few years. I know that $500 a month is not a lot of money compared to some 'big time' investors, but nonetheless, I expect you to treat me exactly as you would them, buying the same quality stocks, bonds, Treasury Bills or whatever and paying as much attention to my portfolio as you would to a millionaire's. When I retire in twenty years or so, I'm sure I'll want to keep investments similar to those I've used to build my portfolio but then, of course, I'll want you to start sending a cheque to me at my condo in Florida every month, making the appropriate deductions for taxes. Oh yes, I'd also like a daily report on the unit value of each investment I own and a full accounting for all purchases, sales and transfers at least annually."

I think we can stop here because the message should be clear. If you were the investment advisor in this example, your only sensible response could be, "There is just one way we can do all those things for you and that is by using mutual funds."

Record of Performance

So far I have not discussed at any length the performance of mutual funds as compared to other investment options. In the next chapter, I will provide some general guidelines on what aspects of performance to consider in choosing a fund or group of funds, but the final selection should be based on more than simple rates of return. What I do want to mention in this chapter, however, on the topic of fund performance, is the amount of information available. As noted several times already, mutual fund prices are published daily in most major newspapers so you can track their progress as frequently as you wish. Additionally, it is possible to obtain, from weekly, monthly or quarterly summaries in those same newspapers, the one-, three- and six-month rates of return as well as the longer term track records for one, two, three, five, and 10 or more years if the fund has been available for that length of time. All mutual fund managers will provide performance data on request for most periods and certainly any good mutual fund advisor will be well acquainted with the results of the various funds they offer (and many that they don't offer). I am not aware of any other investment that makes its performance results so readily available and permits an investor to compare one offering to another with such accuracy. To be sure, the standard caveat applies that "past performance is no guarantee of future results" but, combined with other relevant data, knowing how an investment has performed in the past can definitely improve your chances of selecting one that will come close to meeting your objectives or, conversely, eliminating from consideration those least likely to help you achieve your goals. As mentioned, I'll have more to say about choosing mutual funds in Chapter 12.

Paperwork

Imagine that your portfolio consisted entirely of mutual funds, say, two common stock funds, a bond fund, a real estate fund and a money market fund. And let's further suppose that those funds were all from different managers. In this example, your entire portfolio could be summarized for you on two pieces of paper for each fund – an audited annual financial report of the fund's holdings and transactions and an annual statement of the details of your personal account. Some fund managers prefer to communicate with their unit-holders beyond the minimum requirements of the regulations so you may actually receive many more publications from them but in fact, everything you absolutely need to know about your investments would be contained in those two documents. Contrast that to individually owning the assets represented by the funds. You might have as many as 50 to 100 stocks to keep track of, 10 or 20 bonds, 30 real estate locations and who knows how many Treasury Bills. For each, you would have to document all transactions, account for them annually for tax purposes and tally them all up periodically to see how your portfolio is doing. Isn't owning a mutual fund a simpler way?

Benefits - Peace of Mind

This is one of the basic premises of this book and we began talking about it in the very first pages. At that point, we were referring to the psychological comfort that comes from using an asset allocation approach to investing. Now, however, I want to apply the "peace of mind" notion to mutual funds. The link should be fairly clear — the asset-allocation decisions you made earlier can, in most instances, be implemented entirely through the use of mutual funds. There are funds that match with every *philosophy*, that is, they fit every level of risk tolerance from highly conservative to very aggressive. There are funds to meet every *objective* — liquidity, income or growth — and *asset allocation* can be accomplished among cash, debt and equity funds by making *security selection* form T-Bill, bond, mortgage, dividend, common stock, international, real estate, precious metal, balanced and asset-allocation funds. I am not suggesting that mutual funds are the *only* investment alternative to be considered. I am just repeating my earlier statement that, for most of us, mutual funds are probably the best choice for much of our portfolios.

Taxation

I have begged off discussing taxation in any great detail several times throughout this book because it really is a subject unto itself and could easily fill several hundred pages. However, it is worthwhile to briefly highlight the tax advantage enjoyed by mutual fund investors.

Reducing the taxation issue to its simplest terms, all income realized by an investor is subject to tax with only one exception, that being earnings inside a tax sheltered plan such as a Registered Retirement Savings Plan (RRSP), Registered Pension Plan (RPP), Deferred Profit Sharing Plan (DPSP) or some such special legal arrangement. When we come to discussing the tax advantage of mutual funds, the operative phrase is "income realized" because not all earnings of a mutual fund are immediately realized and thus not immediately taxable. Stick with me on this and I'll try to make some sense of a very complex topic.

Basically, a mutual fund earns profits from three sources: *interest* on the cash balance not invested in specific assets, *dividends* from stocks or interest payments received from bonds and the like in the portfolio and finally, *net capital gains* from any assets sold at a profit. Most mutual funds are structured in such a way that the net amount of those earnings (after fund operating expenses are paid) "flow through" to the investor. The consequence of this "flow through" is that the individual investor, not the fund, is liable for tax. What do not pass on to the investor, however, and are therefore not taxable until received, are the capital gains that have accrued to assets in the portfolio and that have not been sold for profit. I am oversimplifying this description somewhat but it is accurate enough for our needs. Perhaps an example will clarify this a bit.

Suppose you hold units in a hypothetical mutual fund that, at the beginning of the year, had only three assets in its portfolio: $10 million of short-term cash invested in T-Bills, a $10 million government bond and $10 million worth of stock in Apex Corporation. With such a portfolio, the earnings possibilities are:

Asset	Possible Earnings Type
T-Bills	Interest
Bond	Interest and capital gain
Stock	Dividends and capital gain

Let us further assume that about half way through the year, the fund made its only transaction: selling the bond which it purchased for $10 million for $10.1 million. Interest at the rate of 10 percent was earned on the bond up to the date it was sold and the T-Bill holdings also generated interest income of eight percent to the fund. Apex Corporation paid a dividend equivalent to six percent of its beginning-of-the-year share value. The shares of Apex also increased in market value through the year from $10 million to $11.5 million. The fund has 1,500,000 units issued in total and its operating expenses for the year were $500,000. What are the tax consequences under this scenario? The following tabulation shows the earnings and "flow through" to the mutual fund investor.

Income to Mutual Fund

Interest on T-Bill (12 months @ 8%)	$ 800,000
Interest on Bond (6 month @ 10%)	500,000
Capital Gain on sale of Bond	100,000
Dividends from Apex (6% x $10,000,000)	600,000
Total Income	**$ 2,00,000**

Expenses of Mutual Fund

Operating	$ 500,000
Net Income	**$1,500,000**

"Flow through" ($1,500,000/1,500,000 units) $1.00 per unit

If your personal holdings in the fund were 1,000 units, you would receive a tax "slip" for $1,000 ($1.00 x 1000 units). If the legal form of the mutual fund was a "trust," which is the most common, you would receive a T3 and the $1,000 would be proportionately allocated by the fund manager to interest, dividend and capital-gain types of income, which you would correspondingly include on the appropriate line of on your personal tax return. If the mutual fund was set up as a "corporation," all income you receive from it would be reflected on a T5 as "dividend income" or capital gains and would be taxable as such. Note, however, that regardless of the legal form the mutual fund takes, the capital gain from the increase in value of the Apex shares, that is from $10 million to $11.5 million, does not get passed through to you because those gains have not yet been realized. When the stock is ultimately sold by the fund, any resulting profit will be passed along to the unit-holders, but not until then. In this example, the total earnings for each unit were actually $2.50, made up of $1.00 calculated as above plus $1.50 unrealized capital gain. There is, then, a tax deferral advantage associated with mutual fund investing: much of the gain is not taxed until several years down the road when stocks are ultimately sold for profit. Furthermore, capital losses from stocks sold for less than their purchase price will be offset against those gains."

One final point should be made which, although it is not really tax related, does fit in with our comments on distributions from mutual funds. The daily prices shown in the newspapers or quoted elsewhere *include all net earnings of the fund as they occur.* If through the year, for example, a fund had income over and above its expenses of $1.00 per unit and unrealized capital gains of $0.50 per unit, the published unit value would have gradually risen by $1.50. So a fund with a unit value at the start of the year of, say, $5.00, would grow to $6.50 by year's end. If you redeemed the fund just prior to the distribution you would receive $6.50 per unit. If, however, you held onto the fund until its distribution was made, for example, at year end, you would see the published unit value fall by the amount of the distribution. Each year, at the time of annual distributions, mutual fund companies are flooded with calls from investors who want to know why their funds suddenly lost so much value in a single day. In fact, investors didn't lose anything. Using $5.00 as a starting unit value again, if that fund's price rose to $6.50 over the year as interest, dividends and capital gains (realized and unrealized) were reflected and then a distribution of $1.00 per unit were made to flow through the net income earnings to investors, the next day's price in your newspaper would be $5.50 ($6.50 - $1.00). You would be in the same net position because your units would be worth $5.50 plus you would have received $1.00 cash for every unit you owned on the day the distribution was made. Mutual funds accrue all earnings on a daily basis, so when some of those profits are paid out to the unitholders, the price has to fall by the amount of the distribution. In practice, most investors who are not using their mutual funds to provide income take advantage of the "automatic re-investment of distribution" option available from most managers. Under that arrangement, the dollar value of the distributions is used to purchase additional units in the fund. The investor winds up with more units at a lower price, but the total value of his or her investment remains the same as it was prior to the distribution. Whew! Am I glad that's over. I have said far more about tax than I ever intended to and once again, my best advice is to talk to a professional.

Disadvantages

The obvious question I hope you are asking right now is, "Are there any *disadvantages* to owning mutual funds?" And the answer, of course, is "Yes." For one thing, they are boring and they don't serve our need for "bragging rights" particularly well. Repeating the example given earlier in the book, I don't believe there are too many of us who would rush out to tell our friends that our mutual funds just went up a nickel!

Secondly, they all come with fees for the professional management I claim to be so valuable. Even though some funds may call themselves "no load," someone has to pay the people who run and distribute them, so costs are often "buried" in the management fee and so are indirectly reflected in overall performance. That is not to say that some managers don't do a better job of controlling costs than others or that some distributors, particularly large institutions, can't keep costs low by utilizing existing facilities to distribute or manage funds along with all their other products and services. The challenge for you as an investor is to find the right mix of expertise, convenience, variety and performance at a cost that is commensurate with the level of service you desire. For some readers, that will mean engaging a financial planner, full-service broker or product specialist who has the facilities and can afford to respond to your needs for active management of your account. For others who feel they don't require such personal involvement, the services offered by a discount broker, bank teller or phone-in direct marketing firm may be sufficient. Of course, there are many levels in between. Just be sure you understand what you are getting or giving up for the price you pay.

The other major problem with mutual fund investing is that there are simply too many choices. We saw earlier that there are more than 600 funds available in Canada and new ones are being presented every month. Compounding the problem is the fact that not all portfolio managers are created equal so analysis of philosophy, personnel and performance is essential. That is what we are going to do in the next chapter.

Summary

• *Mutual funds are the best investment choice for most Canadians and represent the fastest growing segment of the financial services industry.*

• *Mutual funds developed from three basic investment strategies:*
> *a) pooling of assets,*
> *b) diversification and*
> *c) professional management.*

• *Mutual funds offer the advantages of:*
> *a) liquidity,*
> *b) diversification among assets, asset classes and managers,*
> *c) variety of funds for every objective,*
> *d) flexibility of investment options and payout plans,*
> *e) full time management,*
> *f) short and long term track record and*
> *g) reduced paperwork.*

Chapter Twelve:

Choosing Mutual Funds

THERE ARE NO "ALL WEATHER" MANAGERS WHO
PERFORM WELL UNDER EVERY MARKET CONDITION.

There is a natural tendency, when evaluating mutual funds, to focus attention solely on rate of return as a measure of attractiveness and indeed, most mutual fund companies encourage us to do so with their advertising and promotional material or through the product emphasis they pass along to their distributors, who in turn relay that information to us. I believe, however, that the examination should be a little more encompassing and so I like to consider mutual funds from four perspectives: *Results, risk, rank and resources.*

Results

In the previous chapter, I made the point that the availability of a long-term track record was one of the advantages mutual funds have over other investments. I now need to add a caveat to that statement which is to use *cumulative* performance as a preliminary screen only. It is essential to look at *year-by-year* results to accurately assess a portfolio manager's prowess and the fund's suitability in view of your personal risk tolerance. Let me illustrate with a very simple example. Suppose you had the chance to invest $100 in either of two funds with the following results:

| | Fund A | | Fund B | |
	% Gain	$ Value	% Gain	$ Value
Year 1	+40%	$140	+10%	$110
Year 2	-20%	$112	+13%	$124
Year 3	+25%	$140	+12%	$139
Year 4	+ 4%	$146	+14%	$159
Year 5	+20%	$175	+ 8%	$175

On a cumulative basis, both funds would be worth exactly the same after five years and consequently, their five-year performance would be listed in the various financial information sources as being identical. However, look at the different tracks taken to get to the same result. Fund A did four times as well as Fund B in the first year, twice as well in the third and two-and-a-half times better in the fifth. That would have been exciting! On the other hand, Fund A also lost 20 percent of its value in the second year. That, too, would have been stimulating! I can imagine typical headlines (and advertisements) in the financial press at the end of the first year, – "Hottest Fund in Canada Quadruples Others"– then in the second year – "Has Fund "A" Lost Its Magic?" – to be followed in the third year by something like, "Fund 'A' is Back!" This is an obvious lesson in the danger of looking at short-term performance, good or bad, because as illustrated, there would be no dollar difference had you been in either fund for the full five-year period. But what if you sat on the sidelines through the first year until the media hype convinced you that Fund A was the place to put your money? You might then have jumped in at the beginning of the second year, just in time to watch your investment shrink by 20 percent! Or, suppose you had to redeem your fund at the end of the second year. Fund A would have generated a net return of about six percent annually while Fund B yielded more than 11 percent average per year. And finally, you would have to ask yourself, "Was the excitement of the good years worth the psychological roller coaster ride that came along with it?" I'm not certain that it is and my personal preference would be to avoid funds with inconsistent performance. In fact, let me take a few more lines to illustrate the importance of *consistency* of investment returns.

In his book *The Mutual Fund Wealth Builder,* Michael Hirsch strongly encourages readers to "win by not losing." The reason he is so adamant about "not losing" is that the rate of return required to make up for a loss is much greater than most investors imagine. For example, if you start with $100 and lose 50 percent of it, you have to earn *100 percent* on the remaining $50 to get back to where you were at the beginning. The chart below shows the rates of return needed to overcome various declines.

Loss	Return Required in Next Period to Offset
10%	11%
15%	18%
20%	25%
25%	33%
30%	43%
40%	67%
50%	100%

Notice how the "spread" between the amount of the loss and the required offset widens as the magnitude of the loss is increased. At 10 percent loss, the return needed is only one percent higher; at 15 percent, it is three percent higher; at 20 percent, it is five percent and so on. Large losses are much more difficult to overcome than smaller ones. I can prove that even more convincingly if we think in terms of a target rate of return you might have for your portfolio and the rate you will have to achieve to stay on track if you suffer a significant loss early in the game, say in the first year of a five-year program. As an example from the chart below, we can see that a portfolio constructed to yield an expected return of 10 percent which then loses, say, 15 percent in the first year, must earn 17 percent on average over the next four years to achieve the intended over-

all result. Attempting to achieve that would force you to take on investments with expected return of 17 percent – obviously, much more risky
than those you chose to yield 10 percent.

Annual Gain Needed Next 4 Years		
First Year Loss	10% Target	15% Target
10%	16%	22%
15%	17%	24%
20%	19%	26%
25%	21%	28%
30%	23%	30%
40%	28%	35%
50%	34%	41%

What this means for us in implementing our asset allocation strategy is that we must be as certain as we can be that the overall portfolio
does not suffer significant losses, particularly as our time horizon short-
ens and we have fewer years to overcome any setbacks. Wouldn't that
suggest, therefore, that we should only consider "guaranteed" investments? I hope you have quickly answered "No" to that question or we
haven't made much progress throughout this book. Obviously, if you
could obtain a "guaranteed" investment that would generate sufficient
return to achieve your financial goals, you would choose it. But as we
have proven repeatedly, it is unlikely that the investments that we typically think of as "guaranteed" will, in fact, provide us with the growth we
need to ensure that the purchasing power of our assets remains adequate
through our lifetime. This is the familiar "risk/reward trade-off" and
speaks volumes in favour of diversification to smooth out the peaks and
valleys of investment returns. All investors will experience losses from
time to time. The key to success is to limit those losses to a range that
does not threaten the attainment of your financial goals.

To summarize, when looking at mutual fund performance, do so from three angles: long term, *cumulative* returns as a preliminary assessment of a portfolio manager's expertise; *year-by-year* results as an indication of volatility; and *consistency* to give you some notion of the degree of risk associated with that volatility. All investments, including mutual funds, have some element of risk associated with them. The challenge, as stated previously, is to decide the level of risk you are willing to assume and to understand the implications of that choice. With these thoughts in mind, let's look at the various types of mutual funds and attempt to classify them according to risk.

Risk

I believe mutual funds can be sorted into five distinct categories corresponding to different levels of risk *if we consider risk only in terms of volatility.* For my purposes here, I am ignoring inflation risk and considering only the potential for variability of returns as a measure of risk. On that basis, mutual funds can be grouped from "least risky" to "most risky" as follows:

1. *Cash*
2. *Income*
3. *Balanced*
4. *Growth*
5. *Specialty*

The chart following shows the breakdown for the fund types most commonly available in Canada and it is easy to see that the classification of mutual funds aligns neatly with the three basic asset classes we have used from the beginning. There is not a lot more for me to say about the relationship between the various fund types and their place in your asset allocation decisions because you should apply the same qualification process to mutual funds that you would to any other investment. Think about your *personality, objective* and *time horizon.*

Asset Class	Objective	Fund Type	Description
Cash	Liquidity	Cash	T-Bill
			Money Market
			Cash Management
			Short Term Interest
Debt	Income	Income	Bond
			Mortgage
			Dividend
			Real Estate
Equity	Growth	Growth	Canadian Equity
			U.S. Equity
			Foreign Equity
		Specialty	Precious Metals
			Oil & Gas
			Natural Resources
			High Technology
Combined	Income/ Growth	Balanced	Asset Allocation Balanced

Remember that as you progress from cash-type funds through income to equity and specialty funds, there is a general increase in expected risk and return. In addition, some mutual funds can fall into more than one class and relate to more than one objective. Bond and real estate funds, for example, can generate capital gains as well as income. Growth or specialty funds may yield income in addition to their increase in equity value. Balanced funds and asset allocation funds may fall into any or all of the three classes and objectives, depending on the composition of their portfolios.

Rank

The statement was made previously that "all fund managers are not created equal" and, particularly when it comes to generating returns, all portfolio managers are certainly not blessed with the same talent. Therefore you must look beyond absolute performance to improve your chances of picking the best fund managers for your needs. You must consider the *ranking* of investment managers *relative to their peer group*. It might be great to have a manager who has a track record that gives you confidence in his or her ability to achieve a return over time that will meet your target, but if that level of performance is substantially lower than what other managers with similar funds are achieving, you are taking on more risk than is necessary. If, for example, your target rate of return is 10 percent and the manager you choose achieves that level, you might be satisfied, until you discover that most other managers of similar funds are earning 14 percent. That would mean you were exposing yourself to the same risk for a 10 percent return as your neighbour would be for a 14 percent return. Remember one of our rules from Chapter 8: "All other things being equal, if the risk is the same, choose the investment with the greatest expected return."

As mentioned earlier, there are no "all weather" managers who perform well under every market condition and, in fact, in Canada, despite having over 100 managers from which to choose, there isn't one manager who has ranked in the top ten of the performance charts for each of the past one, three, five and ten year periods. But let's look at a fund with a good 10 year track record which often placed near the top of its peer group. Here are the actual results for the past ten years by that manager:

'Star' Fund Performance

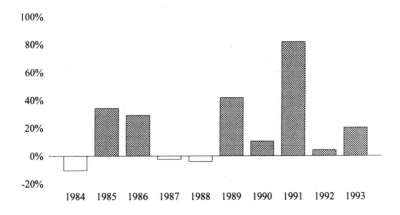

A significant loss in 1984 preceded a modest year and two very good ones. A dramatic decline in 1988 was largely recouped in 1989 only to have the fund lose all that gain the next year until 1991 when it enjoyed a spectacular, industry-leading 81.8 percent increase. The next year saw the return plummet to 4.3 percent and then bounce back to just over 20 percent in 1993. What a ride! This fund has a 10 year average annual return of about 18 percent which is well above its peer group result (which happens to be U.S. equities) of 12 percent. Its three- and five-year numbers are equally impressive. On that basis, then, if U.S. equities were an appropriate asset for your portfolio, you might choose this fund because of its relative ranking. I do hope, however, that the value studying the year-by-year returns is apparent from this example. The volatility of this fund is very high and should be weighed against your risk tolerance. There are other ways to get slightly lower but more stable year-by-year returns. Here are the results of another fund, which also ranks high, although not at the top, of the U.S. equity peer group:

'Almost a Star' Fund Performance

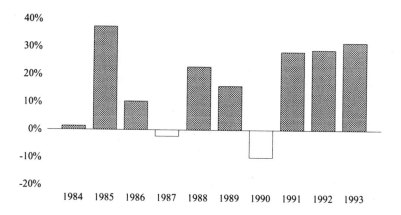

The 10 year average annual return for this fund is approximately 16 percent compared with 18 percent for the previously illustrated one but the volatility is almost half — only ±15 percent compared with ±27 percent. Take your pick — the leader or someone near the top who may not be as spectacular but provides more consistent, above-average returns. Portfolio managers must be ranked according to their risk as well as their returns.

Resources

The final criterion addresses the ability of the fund manager to provide you with the level of expertise and service you require. The first of these, expertise, merits special attention.

If you are going to use performance as any sort of guide to picking mutual funds, you must ensure that the *portfolio manager* in place at the time you buy is the same one who was responsible for the rates of return that attracted you to the fund in the first place. Portfolio managers do, from time to time, change companies although as mentioned, many are often also significant shareholders in their own firms so the tendency is somewhat dampened. However, it does happen that good investment managers retire, die or are attracted away by competitors. This is less of an issue if the particular fund in which you are interested is managed by a *committee* rather than by an individual expert who has attained *star* status with his or her past performance. Under either condition, however, you must determine who was responsible for the fund's track record and whether or not he or she is still in charge. For most investment managers, you should be able to get at least five years' performance history, even if some of that time was spent managing money elsewhere. However, if you are looking at the track record of a manager while he or she was managing another fund, try to compare the type and mandate of the previous fund with the one you are considering. If they are substantially different, you may not be able to rely on the manager's past success being carried forward to the new environment.

The second resource consideration is *service*. Carefully selected, your mutual funds will likely be a part of your investment strategy for many years so it makes sense to deal with an organization that can provide you with the level of service you desire. Some management companies issue monthly reports of transactions and portfolio comments while others provide only the information required annually by regulation. Most funds are available with a range of purchase options, but certain funds may not qualify for all options. Some firms permit full transfers among their own family of funds without charge while others restrict "no fee" movement or assess unit-holders with the cost of making the change. A number of management companies provide toll-free telephone numbers for inquiries. Some insist that you have your signature guaranteed by your banker or sales representative to redeem funds in excess of a certain dollar value while others will accept instructions over the telephone. Certain distributors, such as banks and trust companies, are accessible simply by walking into one of their retail branches whereas most fund managers who distribute through commissioned sales representatives will expect you to deal with your representative rather than directly with them. Not one of these differences is, by itself, good or bad provided you are aware of what you are getting or giving up, as the case may be and certainly, none is critical to the success of your investment program. In evaluating mutual funds, however, it makes sense to look over the whole package.

This completes the list of four criteria I think about when considering mutual funds for my portfolio: returns, risk, rank and resources. Before we wind up this chapter (and the book), there are just a couple more things about mutual funds we should consider.

How Many Funds Should I Own?

There is no standard answer to this question because the size of your portfolio, combined with your personal objective and risk tolerance, will have an impact on the decision. Consequently, what is right for you may not be best for me. It would be reasonable to say, however, given some of the things we have covered in this book about diversification, that the greater the diversity among funds you have, the more likely you will be able to avoid major losses in overall portfolio values. It also seems prudent to respond to the increasing volatility of markets with a broader range of investments.

To simplify this discussion, I will assume that your entire portfolio will be comprised of mutual funds even though, for most readers, that will not be so. If that were the situation, however, as a minimum, you should have all three asset classes represented by different funds, which would require you to own at least three funds. The alternative, of course, is to buy a balanced fund or an asset allocation fund and have it represent all three classes for you, which, if your portfolio isn't too large or if you have a "passive money manager" personality, may be just the thing to do. The shortcoming of those types of funds, however, is that you are still relying on only one portfolio manager and the "mix" of investments is usually restricted, eliminating the possibility to personally tailor your portfolio in any way.

On the other hand, if your portfolio is sufficiently large or you want to take a more active role in the management of your money, even three funds may not be enough. Let's say, for example, you elected to have 30 percent of your portfolio in Canadian equities. If you used only one manager and he or she had a bad year, 30 percent of your portfolio would suffer. Why not diversify among two or three Canadian equity managers so that if one underperforms, only 10 or 15 percent of your assets will be affected?

Can you own too many funds? Certainly you can for a number of reasons, the most important of which is the potential for duplication of investments. There is little value in owning, for example, three income funds that are all invested in the same bonds. If all of your income fund managers are buying the same bonds, there is no diversification effect. As a general rule of thumb, look at the top 10 holdings in each fund and if you see at least 25 percent overlap, think about consolidating the funds or substituting a manager with a different outlook.

Another consequence of holding too many funds is that you defeat one of the advantages of mutual funds: reduced paperwork. You might also be incurring duplicate transaction costs or trustee fees, in the case of RRSPs.

To provide an example of a broadly diversified mutual fund portfolio, I have taken the "tree diagram" developed at the end of Chapter 9 and used funds exclusively. The result is a collection of 10 different funds. Obviously, this works best for a large portfolio but the concept building a "multi-fund portfolio" can be applied to any reasonable dollar amount.

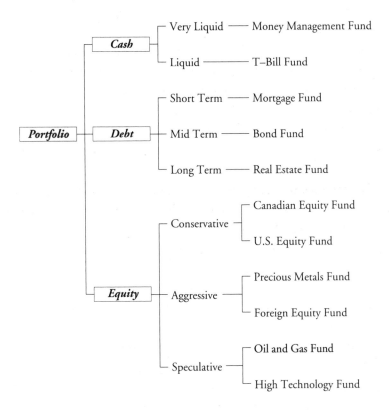

How Do I Get My Money Out?

With this question, I am not talking about simply cashing in your funds. That is a straightforward administrative process which is easily accomplished. Here I am referring back to that section in Chapter 10 that deals with converting your accumulated assets into regular income. For purposes of clarity, I am going to avoid distinguishing between Registered Retirement Income Funds (RRIFs) and "non-registered" investments. The RRIF has a "minimum income rule" which has some bearing on what you can and cannot do to meet your income needs but the strategy for getting to your money on a regular basis is essentially the same. Nor am I going to discuss the tax aspects of this procedure. Both of those topics should be reviewed with a competent advisor.

One of the most under-used mutual fund products is the *withdrawal plan*. Perhaps its name has something to do with that — it sounds painful! Yet in reality, the automatic withdrawal arrangement is the most intelligent and flexible method for converting assets into income. Quite simply, it works like this: you invest your money in a mutual fund or group of funds and then ask the manager or managers to send you a cheque on a regular basis. You determine the amount of the cheque and the frequency and you can increase (or decrease) the payout at any time. You don't have to worry about whether your portfolio is generating interests from its debt-type holdings or dividends and capital gains from your equities. The fund manager simply redeems a sufficient number of your units each period to provide whatever amount of cash you have requested.

Why would this be of benefit? Recall my comments very early in this book about the danger of abandoning equities in favour of "less risky" investments such as bonds as you approach retirement. The consequence is erosion of purchasing power due to inflation. Yet as a practical matter if you have all of your money invested in the stock market, for example, how do you arrange things so that you can receive a regular income from those assets? I don't think your stockbroker would welcome your instruction (every month) to "sell fifteen shares of my IBM stock and send me a cheque for $1,000." The natural tendency, therefore, is to think about changing growth assets into income-producing ones. The problem with that strategy, as we already know, is that you will lower the overall portfolio rate of return. But by utilizing a mutual fund withdrawal plan, you don't have to do that.

If you are happy with the portfolio mix you had prior to retirement, you needn't change it to have a greater weighting of income-producing assets. You instruct the management company as to which funds you want to systematically redeem and how much is to be withdrawn from each. The fund manager then automatically converts a portion of your holdings to cash each month and sends it off to you. The only concern you should have is that the portfolio continues to earn sufficient return to provide the level of income you desire. In setting the level of redemption, you have to consider the things we talked about in Chapter 10. Recall my suggestion there that you try to limit the annual withdrawals to the difference between the portfolio's overall return and the rate of inflation. But beyond that and the tax implications any "cashing in" of investments, the withdrawal plan idea is a sound one. You don't have to alter your portfolio at retirement although you are free to do so then or at any time later. What remains in the portfolio after each withdrawal continues to compound at the same rate of return in would if you were not touching the money. That allows you to increase your withdrawal amounts as you go. Below is an illustration of the actual results for a well-known small cap growth fund where an initial amount of $100,000 was invested in 1974 and $1,000 per month, that is, 12 percent annually of the original amount, is withdrawn. The withdrawals were then increased by 5 percent per year. There is also a column showing the result of the withdrawal had an alternative investment yielding 15 percent been used. Note that the fund had negative returns in four years (1981, 1984, 1987 and 1990) yet the value of the fund is still *seventeen times* the amount of the original investment *and* $366,000 has been withdrawn. Please also be aware that this example is simplified to illustrate the concept.

Date	Annual Return	Annual Withdrawals	Total Withdrawals	Remaining Cash Value	15% Investment
1974	n/a	n/a	n/a	$100,000	$100,000
1975	41.6%	$12,000	$12,000	129,129	103,000
1976	33.7	12,600	24,600	119,913	105,850
1977	23.6	13,224	37,824	181,113	108,504
1978	30.9	13,896	51,720	221,603	110,883
1979	53.5	14,592	66,312	322,040	112,923
1980	53.1	15,324	81,636	462,903	114,538
1981	-11.4	16,092	97,728	395,315	115,627
1982	38.2	16,896	114,624	524,712	116,075
1983	33.3	17,736	132,360	681,185	115,750
1984	-0.2	18,624	150,984	660,324	114,488
1985	34.9	19,560	170,544	868,780	112,102
1986	9.7	20,544	191,088	932,813	108,373
1987	-2.4	21,576	212,664	891,292	103,053
1988	8.9	22,656	235,320	947,883	95,855
1989	21.2	23,784	259,104	1,125,061	86,449
1990	-5.4	24,972	284,076	1,038,034	74,444
1991	41.9	26,220	310,296	1,442,033	59,391
1992	11.7	27,528	337,824	1,579,494	40,772
1993	9.5	28,908	366,732	1,698,561	17,979

In all likelihood, in this scenario the investor would have increased the amount of the monthly withdrawals even more as the years passed and it became evident that the fund was growing at a rate faster than it was being depleted by the income payout. By 1993, for example, a $29,000 withdrawal represented less than two percent of the total fund value.

Obviously I chose a fund with a very good long-term track record to dramatize my point; however, I believe the convenience and flexibility of a mutual fund withdrawal plan is clear. All of the features, advantages and benefits of mutual funds that make so much sense in the accumulation of wealth can be continued through the conversion of that wealth to income.

Summary

- *Mutual funds should be evaluated by:*
  a) Short and long term rate of return,
  b) Risk *of volatility,*
  c) Rank *among peers and*
  d) Personnel and technological resources
- *Use cumulative performance as a preliminary screen only. Look at year-by-year results to accurately assess a portfolio manager's prowess and the fund's suitability in view of your personal risk tolerance.*
- *The rate of return required to make up for a loss is much greater than most investors imagine.*
- *There are no "all weather" managers who perform well under every market condition.*
- *As a minimum, have all three asset classes represented by different funds or buy an asset allocation fund and have it represent all three classes for you.*
- *Study the top 10 holdings in each fund and if you see at least 25 percent overlap, think about consolidating the funds or substituting a manager with a different outlook.*
- *The automatic withdrawal arrangement is the most intelligent and flexible method for converting assets into income.*

Conclusion

If I have been successful in my mission, you will now share my belief that it is possible to "get a piece of the action with peace of mind." Managing your money need not be complicated but nor is it easily accomplished. We can legitimately say that accumulating wealth is a relatively straight-forward process because the few principles of successful investing that are important are also fairly easy to understand. On the other hand, the questions that have to be answered sometimes seem to have no right or wrong response. For example, we know that the two greatest risks to investors are inflation and volatility of returns but to the extent you struc-ture your portfolio to avoid one, it unfortunately becomes exposed to the other. You must, therefore, decide which risk is the greater one for you.

Time horizon is a critical factor and the one that brings into focus the trade-off between risk and reward. Short-time-horizon portfolios require cash or debt-type assets to preserve principal values while longer-term perspectives are best served with inflation-fighting assets such as equities. The concept of broad diversification as a risk-reduction strategy, however, applies to all time frames.

Risk is a "four letter word" because it implies uncertainty, which investors don't like. Yet uncertainty in investing cannot be avoided and in fact, it is the engine that drives returns. The greater the risk – the greater the expected return should be. Initially, your individual ability to tolerate risk is shaped by past experience but it can change over time as you gain new knowledge that affects your investment personality.

Your investment personality and your risk tolerance combine to form a philosophy that becomes the cornerstone for an Investment Statement. Objectives are set, assets allocated and securities selected within a frame of reference that leads to greater equanimity and staying power – both of which are vital for successful investing.

Despite the pretense of ease with which I have described the development of an investment strategy, I know that "easier said than done" applies. It is one thing to intellectually understand the concepts presented and quite another to implement and adhere to principles over the long term that periodically place you at odds with much of the investing public, not to mention human nature itself. Try though. Try as best you can to be "approximately right rather than precisely wrong." Your sound judgement and perseverance will be rewarded many times over.

Couldn't someone you know benefit from reading *Risk Is a Four Letter Word — The Asset Allocation Approach to Investing*? It makes a great gift — one that you will be thanked for many times because it is understandable, enjoyable and most of all, practical.

Please rush me _____ copies of *Risk Is a Four Letter Word* at a special price of $17.95 each (including GST and shipping). I have enclosed a cheque made payable to Hartman & Company Inc. in the amount of $_____.

Full Name:

Address:

City: Province:

Postal Code: Telephone: (   )

For an order of 10 or more books, we offer a discount.
Please write, call or fax us for details.

Hartman & Company Inc.
Suite 300, 1497 Marine Drive
West Vancouver, B.C. V6T 1B8
Telephone: (604) 926-3623
Facsimile: (604) 925-1430